BIRJU MAHARAJ

BIRJU MAHARAJ

The Master Through My Eyes

Saswati Sen

NIYOGI BOOKS

Published by

NIYOGI BOOKS

Block D, Building No. 77,
Okhla Industrial Area, Phase-I,
New Delhi-110 020, INDIA
Tel: 91-11-26816301, 26818960
Email: niyogibooks@gmail.com
Website: www.niyogibooksindia.com

Design: Write Media

ISBN: 978-93-81523-82-7
Year of Publication: 2013

Printed at: Niyogi Offset Pvt. Ltd., New Delhi, India

CONTENTS

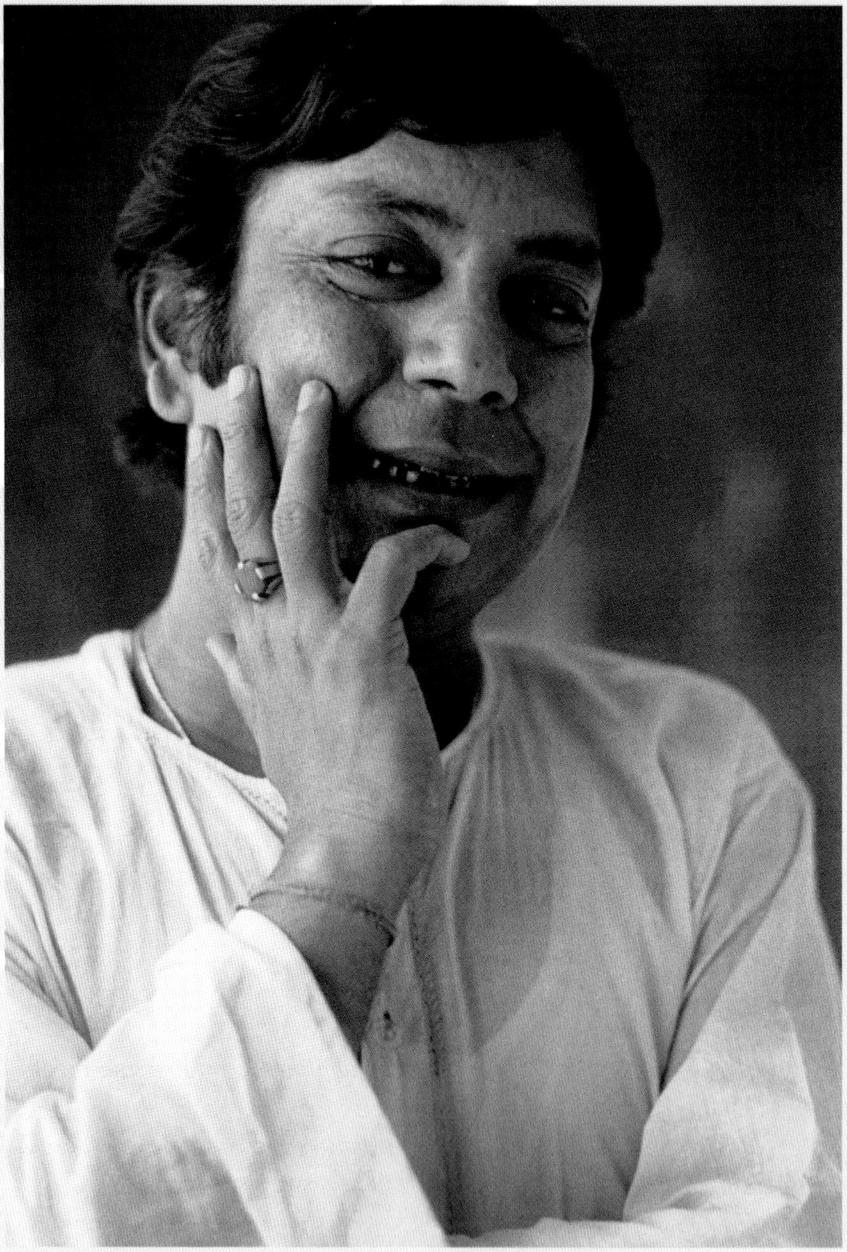

A cheerful Birju Maharaj in his forties.

FOREWORD

Perhaps this would be the first book on me that is written with a deep insight into every aspect of my life and work. After many decades of study and observation, Saswati has been able to capture my innermost thoughts and feelings. She has taken these experiences and penned them into this heartfelt memoir.

Even as a child when she was under the tutelage of Reba Didi I could see a commitment in her towards art. Her total dedication and surrender gave me the opportunity to mould her the way a potter moulds clay into a beautiful pot. *Taal, ang, abhinaya,* in all these facets of dance, she has seen and absorbed my training with thorough and complete understanding. She has trained with me as a performer, a teacher, a choreographer and an adept stage presenter. Her hard work and efforts are now the driving force behind my institute, Kalashram.

I am very happy to extend my blessings for the success of this book and its author, my loving disciple, Saswati Sen.

Pandit Birju Maharaj

At the Golden Gate Bridge, San Francisco, in the eighties.

PREFACE

Bharatiya Kala Kendra, Mata Sundari Road, New Delhi. A young dance student, dedicated to her learning, hurries through the sprawling lawns to reach her dance class on time. She gets a strange feeling as several eyes move with her and whispers get loud, though not discernible. She is aware that they are talking about her. A quick glance over her shoulder, and she rushes into the classroom.

My first dance teacher, Reba Chatterjee Vidyarthy, or Didi, as we called her, was probably the most caring and hardworking teacher for beginners and young aspirants. I was one of her most sincere students. Learning dance gave me great joy. However, the unsettling episode with the 'whispering group' kept repeating itself and soon I began finding ways to avoid class or change my timings or even my route.

In 1969, I was awarded the National Scholarship by the Ministry of Culture and this led me to seriously think about dance as a secondary profession (though my family dreamt of my becoming a doctor). Didi delivered me under the tutelage of a senior guru from the *gharana* (school of music or dance), and suddenly, there I was, in front of the person who I had dreaded confronting the most—the same person who seemed to be the leader of the 'whispering group' who used to talk about me while I was on my way to class!

Maharajji (later I came to know him as Pandit Birju Maharaj) welcomed me warmly and spoke highly about my seemingly bright future career. He told Didi how he and the others such as Pradeep Bhai and Pratap Bhai always appreciated my commitment towards learning and the humble appearance that I bore. None of this really moved me to shed a sense of wariness. My friends envied me for this great opportunity but I remained passive in class. I made it very clear within the first few days that I was unhappy to be in his class and would be happier if sent back to Didi. However, that would probably have meant forgoing my scholarship. Painstakingly, Maharajji tried to pull me out of my shell for some time. Finally, one day, he let me go, saying: '*Man kare toh aana, par nakhre mat dikhao*' (Come if your heart is in it, but don't expect me to bear your tantrums).

I kept going to class and watched him teach Surama Gandharias, a Uruguayan student, and other seniors, for almost six months. Craving to learn and dance, I realised what I would lose—Maharajji's teaching was wonderful, with minute attention to detail for every movement, body line and expression.

Finally, one day I gained the courage to apologise for my behaviour and stood up to learn. Since that day, there has been no looking back. Maharajji's teaching was so perfect, so analytical, so interesting, that anyone could almost immediately experience the aesthetic beauty that it holds. We spent days learning and correcting each piece (*tukra/tihai/aamad*) that he taught. Hearing a word of appreciation from him (with which he was miserly in those days!) was like an achievement. Our training moved gradually with no hurry or immediate targets to meet. Both Surama and I enjoyed learning the challenging patterns of technique and the subtlety in execution. Our passions were similar towards dance and our goal was humble—a satisfying smile on our mentor's face.

Analysing the present day scenario of learning, it surprises me how drastically it has changed with one generation. The most interesting method about Maharajji's teaching is the way he co-relates every rhythmic phrase and its corresponding movement or footwork with a simile or a known action. This easy method of teaching students has also helped in reaching the uninitiated audience.

As a child I had witnessed a few Kathak performances, most of which left an impression in my mind about the dance being full of fast footwork, pirouettes and undefined brisk movements, quite obviously different from the three other main forms—Kathakali, Bharatnatyam and Manipuri—all of which had clear, graceful lines and stances. Maharajji was working on giving the form an elegant, picturesque look. While teaching and correcting, he humorously referred to the plight of the poor photographer who only wanted to make some quick money by taking a few pictures of the dancer performing, which he never really could, as there was no point of freeze. I remember how excited we were, nearly three decades ago, when for the first time we saw some beautiful poses photographed while *in action*. I developed a deep admiration towards his training methods (a process which continues till this day).

As I compile memories of the last fifty years in this book, I see the aura of a great man—my guru—even through my closed eyes. An icon of Indian dance, a living legend, a mentor for thousands, an inspiration for countless people across the globe, Pandit Birju Maharaj is an unassuming, simple person outside his artistic world. Though I know him well, I am unsure whether I can do justice in describing this divine personality. *Birju Maharaj: The Master Through My Eyes* is my tribute to a great man who, among his many stellar accomplishments, spread awareness of the classical dance form that is Kathak, not only in India, but abroad, while changing innumerable lives along the way.

A powerful dance posture.

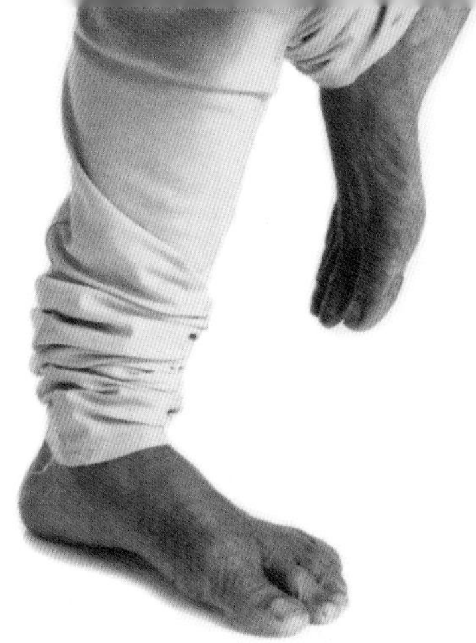

THE GREAT HERITAGE

Born to Achhan Maharajji and Mahadeiji on 4 February 1938 was their eighth child, a baby boy. In the maternity ward of Balrampur Hospital, Lucknow, this was the only male child amid many females born on that day. A neighbour immediately suggested an appropriate name—Brij Mohan—the enchanter of Brij (Lord Krishna). After his birth, his mother was very ill and often became rather moody, sometimes to the extent of even resenting his birth (which of course she regretted with tears in her later life). However, under the loving care of his three sisters—Badi Jeeya (elder sister) Vidyavati, Sutto Jeeya (middle sister) Saraswati, Chhoti Jeeya (little sister) Chandravati—Babuji (father), Chachaji (uncle) and others, the baby Birju, as he was lovingly called, grew to develop a great passion and understanding for dance and music right from his cradle days. He often crawled up to the *talimkhana* (training room) where his father taught and spent hours enjoying the music.

When his son was about a year old, Achhan Maharajji got an invitation from Raja Ram Nagar in Kolkata. His mother, Ammaji, little Birju and Sevakmama (his maternal uncle) accompanied him. They lived in a rented house at Bowbazar. One day, in a mischievous mood, the baby crawled up the stairs and hid under the cot that belonged to the landlady, an Anglo-Indian woman. After hours of search and anguish, they finally found him having a great time enjoying his pocketful of goodies. Sevakmama, who had lived with them all his life, got a scolding from his sister for being neglectful.

A year later, the family migrated to Raigarh at the invitation of Raja Chakradhar Singh. Here, Achhan Maharajji was engaged as the court dancer and to teach three to four of the Raja's favourites: Kartik Ram, Kalyan Das, Firtooji and Burmanji. Jai Lalji of the Jaipur style was also in the Raja's court.

Achhan Maharajji was then invited to the court of the Nawab of Rampur. It was here that the Nawab Sahib, Raza Ali, engaged the little Birju to serve as a dancer in the court along with his father. The Rampur durbar had great masters on their rolls such as Ustad Mushtaque Hussain for vocals, Ustad Hafiz Ali Khan Sahib for the sarod, Janab Ahmed Jan Thirakwa for the tabla and Pandit Ayodhya Prasad for the pakhawaj. Nawab Sahib Raza Ali and his father Nawab Hamid Ali were connoisseurs and patrons of the arts and often hosted great performances. They loved to watch young Birju dance before his father's performance. As part of their regular duty Achhan Maharajji and his son were supposed to report at the palace durbar at around seven in the evening. Often they were asked to go back as there was no *mehfil* (gathering). At times the Nawab called for the artists to perform any time of the day or night. The poor little child would then be forced to wake up, get dressed in a *sherwani* and *topi* (knee-length coat and cap) and prepare for dancing with half-sleepy eyes. Many times he had tears in his eyes as Sutto Jeeya applied his make-up—*kajal* (eyeliner) and *tika* (coloured mark on the forehead).

Coming back to Lucknow occasionally was enjoyable for the child. He engaged in games with his friends—flying kites, playing *kancha* (marbles), sneaking into cinema halls and running about the streets. His grandmother was afraid that he would hurt himself while chasing falling kites and collecting the string. She helped him find measures to play safely. When he was just four years old his grandmother (widow of Kalka Maharajji) passed away. The child was unhappy for days, as she used to tell him stories and he would share many little secrets with her. She also told him about his illustrious ancestors, all of whom were great artists and contributed to the enrichment of Kathak.

For basic studies Maharajji went to the elementary school near his house at Jhau Lal Pul; but studies, of course, did not interest him in the least. Often he would make an excuse and run out to fly kites with his friends. They has some very interesting names for the kites—*Chand Tara* (for the moon and stars design); *Bherial* (for curly designs on the borders); *Tankhia* (for the kites with a 'U' or half-moon pattern on top); *Patti Daar* (for those with a diagonal strip); *Chap* (for kites that were divided into different colours) and *Paesalchi* (for those that were small in size and worth one paisa only). It was difficult to prepare the *manja-dori* (string) with glue and glass powder and Maharajji's fingers were always cut on the sides, which itched or caused him pain while he ate his food. If he ran out of money, he would go to the nearby kite shop of Babban Bhai and entertain him with his dance to get a free kite. If by luck a kite fell on the rooftop or nearby treetop, there was great reason to celebrate.

Maharajji remembers an incident that took place on the first anniversary of India's Independence—15 August 1948—when all the roads were decorated with banners and flags. In the evening the children were running about collecting these. Maharajji's best friends in the neighbourhood were Jagat, Lallu, Bhagoti, Nasir, Jayram, Manu, Hanuman and Jogu Bhaiya. He was quite a hero among them, as his artistic qualities were admired right from the beginning. Maharajji and these friends were busy collecting kites from the street and in the dark he failed to notice a broken glass bottle strewn with the sharp edge up. He stepped right into it with his left foot. Afraid of being scolded at home, his friends managed to get some cloth and cotton wool and tied it to stop the bleeding. It was only in the morning that his mother discovered the injury. He was given a scolding for being neglectful since he would be unable to practise dance for quite a few days.

Maharajji enjoyed singing film songs and imitated many Bollywood singers. He loved Talat Mehmood's deep, melodious and sonorous voice. His favourite songs were *Dil Leke Chale To Nahin Jaoge, Tasveer Banata Hoon, Jalte Hain Jiske Liye, Aye Mere Dil Kahin Aur Chal, Aa Jayo Tadapte Hain Armaan, Gaye Jaa Geet Milan Ke, Din Khushion Ke, Mehfil Mein Jal Uthi Shama, Na Kisiki Aankh Ka Noor Hoon* and *Dharti Ko Aakash Pukare.* He soon became very popular in the neighbourhood and was also much in demand for singing for the women folk during festivals and household ceremonies. He sang as he played the *dholak* (drum) folk style.

In those days there were quite a few Sindhi and Punjabi families in the neighbourhood, some of whom Maharajji remembers and still connects with very fondly. Vijay Kumar, who is settled in New York since the past thirty years, is one of his dearest friends and it is amazing to see them bonding whenever they meet. Baghi, who used to be their neighbour, from a Sindhi family, is another person he remembers with love and respect, as she was very helpful and caring during the days of their poverty and struggle. Many times she would quietly prepare some food and bring it to him, knowing that he was probably hungry. He never met her after her marriage in the fifties.

Achhan Maharajji was gentle in nature so his son had no fear in sharing his mischievous escapades with him, including his attempts at puffing cigarettes. But Maharajji's uncle, Shambhu Maharajji, was very strict and tolerated no nuisance. Once, when he was out of town, Maharajji quietly joined a young boys' social group, Swasthya Kendra, Golaganj, and accepted to dance as a female character in one of their street plays. His uncle returned home before schedule and gave the little Birju quite a spanking for taking on this role.

Maharajji loved to watch Hindi films and his favourite heroines were Suraiya and Nimmi. On many occasions he was caught trying to imitate the tones and dialogues of film heroes. His uncle did not approve of this and his punishment was to call the barber to cut off Maharajji's hair, making it small and spiky. On the other hand, Maharajji was pampered a lot by the women folk in his home—his mother, sisters and Chachi (aunt). He would act like Chachaji, puffing on the hookah and make his Chachi press his legs. Sutto Jeeya, however, was his favourite and he obeyed her the most.

After primary school at Jhau Lal Pul, Maharajji got admission in Sentinial High School for a short period and later in Vidyant Hindu Inter College. Here again his reluctance to study placed him in humiliating situations, especially as the girl who sat next to him always stood first. The English teacher would be mad at him and pull his ears. The tutor at home (Baiji) also struggled without much results to help him in English. However, he excelled in music and was quite popular with his classmates and seniors as a result of singing *Vande Mataram* soulfully.

Around the time when Maharajji was seven years old, the family left Rampur for Delhi, as Shrimati Nirmala Joshi invited Achhan Maharajji to work at the Hindustani School of Music and Dance (the present Sangeet Bharati). Shrimati Kapila Malik (now Vatsyayan), Shrimati Leela Kripalani, Shrimati Usha Bhatia and Shri GR Gupta were some of the prominent students there. The young Birju would accompany his father to class daily where he eagerly observed his training and learnt faster than most of the students. He memorised long dance compositions effortlessly. His father was always proud of his talent and foresaw a great genius in him—a thought that he often shared with his wife.

1947, the year of India's partition and the Hindu-Muslim riots, was horrific. Delhi being the target of crime and high risk, Achhan Maharajji's family hastily returned to Lucknow. They had to leave quietly in the dead of night with the help of some faithful supporters. Life in Lucknow had to start afresh and to earn a living Achhan Maharajji often performed in several small towns and villages during festive occasions, as also in the houses of rich landlords during joyous family celebrations such as marriage, childbirth and so on.

The young Birju danced mostly before his father's main programme. Once, when he was less than nine years old, he played the tabla for his father at a conference in Kolkata. He also performed at the house of a *tawaif* (dancing professional) in Kolkata. The hall was full with women who were truly devoted and great connoisseurs of the arts. After the performance he received immense appreciation and a lot of gifts (gold chain, rings, money and so on). Along with his father and Chachaji he performed at a conference where he was given the best dancer prize and was proud to have excelled among his seniors.

In celebration of this small happiness, his father gave him a glass of sweetened *bhang* (intoxicant made from leaves and flowers). Within no time the little boy was reeling and could not sit up straight. Seeing this, Chachaji was very upset and gave them a piece of his mind. The next morning Achhan Maharajji woke up early and sent little Birju to press Chachaji's body while he was still in bed. Chachaji lovingly excused him.

Along with his father, the young Birju performed in Kanpur, Patna, Kolkata, Mumbai, Jaunpur, Mainpuri, Gorakhpur, Allahabad, Buxar, Balia and Muzaffarpur. In the summer of 1947, when Achhan Maharajji went for a programme to Mainpuri, the extreme heat and inadequate facilities made him feel very uneasy. By the evening he was down with high fever and unable to perform properly. That was when the little Birju had to represent him and the child stole the show. They returned to Lucknow where his father's condition became worse and finally he died of brain haemorrhage.

The family was completely shocked and their financial condition turned bleak. The little boy was only nine-and-a-half years old and there was no earning member in the family. Partition had just taken place and not much was happening in the field of performing arts. Even while they were in mourning, the young Birju had to accept two unimpressive programmes to be able to collect enough money to perform his father's last rites.

Still from a documentary by C Dasgupta.

START OF A LEGACY

The Kathakar's tradition started in the Hadia district, near Sultanpur in Uttar Pradesh. The extended family initially lived in Hariya Tehsil where it is believed that nine hundred and eighty-nine families of the Kathak *beradari* (clan) stayed together, earning a living from singing and dancing in village temples and also through agriculture. The style of dance was very simple—a storytelling tradition enhanced through rhythm and movements. The literary content, however, was rich. It was mainly an oral tradition passed on from one generation to the next. Ishwari Prasadji is considered the earliest practitioner of this style of dancing and to him goes the credit of carrying forward a formal, defined style, which gradually blossomed with each passing generation.

Famines and epidemics forced this family to leave the village and thus they reached Lucknow with the help of Tikait Ramji, a clergyman working with the Nawab's administrative staff. Soon their extraordinary talent was recognised by the Nawab and they were respectfully employed as the jewels of the court during the time of Nawab Asaf-ud-Daula. Later, during Nawab Wajid Ali Shah's reign, Thakur Prasadji and Durga Prasadji and later Bindadin Maharajji and Kalka Maharajji received immense support and patronage. Nawab Wajid Ali Shah, an ardent lover of poetry, music and dance, also took inspiration and guidance from the masters to compose several beautiful dance presentations with his many wives and concubines. *Rahas* and *Indrasabha* were among his favourite compositions.

1857 was a dark period, when India's First War of Independence broke out and Lucknow was under siege. The family—Bindadin Maharajji, Kalka Maharajji, his wife—

and a few trusted workers fled the city to seek safer surroundings. They travelled for days on foot and other basic means of transport and finally reached Bhopal almost like refugees. Within a few days, the neighbourhood came to know about their artistic prowess and genius through their daily *riyaz* (practice). Word reached the palaces and they were invited respectfully to present their art. The queens were particularly impressed by the beauty of their dance and almost every evening they performed for the royal household and their guests. As they did not have many formal clothes, the Begum regularly ordered new dresses for them. The family stayed in Bhopal and enjoyed the royal hospitality for several months only to return to Lucknow when it became peaceful.

Bindadin Maharajji's dance was very elegant and forceful, as he had great command over rhythm. His *abhinaya* (expression) was also rich and emotive. It is said that he once danced through the whole night in the Nawab's court, unfolding countless ways of describing and portraying only one verse of a *thumri* (genre of semi-classical Indian music)—*Balma re chunariya maika laal ranga de* (Oh! my beloved, please colour my scarf red).

Kalka Maharajji's dance was graceful and lyrical. His *bhav* (emotion) was subtle and captivating. Kalka Maharajji had three sons—Shri Jagannath Prasad (Achhan Maharajji), Shri Baijnath Prasad (Lachhu Maharajji) and Shri Shambhu Nath (Shambhu Maharajji)—all of whom were extremely talented. Most of their training was under the strict guidance of their *Bade Abba* (elder uncle), Bindadin Maharajji, who spent long hours teaching Achhan Maharajji and allowed no breaks, not even for food. Kalka Maharajji died young, around the age of forty-five, but Bindadin Maharajji lived till over eighty years. After his death, the family's lavish style of living started to decline and Lucknow also lost its royal touch. Achhan Maharajji felt orphaned as he was in the prime of his *talim* (training) at the age of forty. He was an extraordinary genius in the *layakari* (rhythmic) aspect of the art. So good was his command that he could speak rhythmic compositions in three to four *taal*s (claps in rhythmic pattern) simultaneously. Though big built, his dance was effortless and graceful. His wrist movements were supple, the execution of footwork patterns had beauty and style and his entire body was lyrical. The speciality of his *bhav batana* (a composition where emotion dominates) was in the quick changes, varieties of expressions and hand movements. Unique were his *mayur* (peacock), *mahout* (elephant rider), *aanchal* (scarf) and *naao* (boat) movements, which the other brothers dared not perform. Both the younger brothers mostly learnt under him and had tremendous respect and love for him, as he was a gentle, humble and giving person.

Lachhu Maharajji was the most fashionable and handsome among the brothers. His style was delicate and soft, particularly in the portrayal of women, which made one quiver. The uniqueness of his *bhav* was the rare similes he captured; he carried the audience into deep imagination. As a young boy, he once accompanied his seniors to a performance at the house of a rich landlord, but the petty arrangements and ill treatment from the hosts made him furious and he promised never to return to such an environment. He left for Kolkata and worked at New Theatres during the time of Rai Chand Boral and other stalwarts. He lived in style in expensive houses and drove around in cars. From here he went to the Mumbai film industry. His contribution to dance choreography in films will remain immortal through some of the famous compositions in *Mughal-e-Azam, Pakeeza, Teesri Kasam* and others. In the nineties, Lachhu Maharajji returned to Lucknow after a successful tenure in Mumbai and started teaching regularly at the Kathak Kendra there, which he continued until his death.

Shambhu Maharajji, the youngest, was dark and tall with a dancer's body. His large intoxicating eyes and his striking personality were the envy of many. As a young boy he was fascinated by the tabla and took it very seriously, until his elder brother found ways of creating more interest in him towards the family profession of dance. His dance was powerful and masculine, so much so that often while performing on makeshift stages, the platforms gave way under the force of his strong stamping. Amid his footwork patterns, he excelled in the execution of *Na dhin dhin na*—an imitation of the tabla rendering. His *abhinaya* was extremely moving and the audience would get carried away by his captivating eyes, which made many hearts cry. His *gat-nika*s (stance with stylised gait) were famous, particularly—*ghunghat, rukhsar* and *husna.* He also had good training in vocal music. Nearly every evening, friends and artists gathered in the courtyard of their house in Lucknow to enjoy and share rich music under the famous guava tree. Great musicians such as Shrimati Begum Akhtar, Pandit Bhimsen Joshi and Shrimati Siddheswari Devi admired his music immensely. Shambhu Maharajji had a very powerful personality; even those who were close to him were afraid of him, as he tolerated no nonsense. But in his heart he was very helpful and caring. While in Lucknow, all the neighbours knew that they could walk in for assistance, especially if any medical assistance was needed. He knew the senior doctors at Balrampur Hospital, who had great admiration for him and never refused help. There was also this incident about a thief who had entered a neighbour's house at night and was caught as he was about to escape. The policemen handcuffed him and dragged him through the lanes. Hearing the commotion Shambhu Maharajji

Still from Shatranj-ke-Khilari *depicting Nawab Wajid Ali Shah's court.*

peeped out and asked that the thief be brought in. He patiently heard all that had happened and then requested the policemen to let the thief go after a stern warning. He also applied some first aid on the thief's wound.

Shambhu Maharajji went to Kolkata very often and had lots of friends and admirers there. He taught quite a few students in Kolkata—the more prominent ones being Shrimati Bandana Sen, Pandit Ram Narain Misra, Shri Krishna Maharaj and Shrimati Maya Chatterjee. Some celebrities and film actors such as Pahari Sanyal, Chhaya Devi, RC Boral, Chinmay Lahiri and KC Dey were his close friends. He migrated to Delhi in the fifties and began teaching at Bharatiya Kala Kendra, which was initially at Shrimati Sumitra Charat Ram's house and later at Firoz Shah Kotla. Several other great masters also taught here—Ustad Hafiz Ali Khan and the senior Dagar Brothers (Fahim-ud-dinji and Amin-ud-dinji). He lived with his wife, Phulkumari and three children (Rameswari, Krishan Mohan and Ram Mohan) at Pusa Road. Shambhu Maharajji passed away on 4 November 1969 at the All India Medical Institute of Sciences, New Delhi. He had cancer of the throat. On his death hundreds of students and admirers from all over the country paid their tribute to the great master.

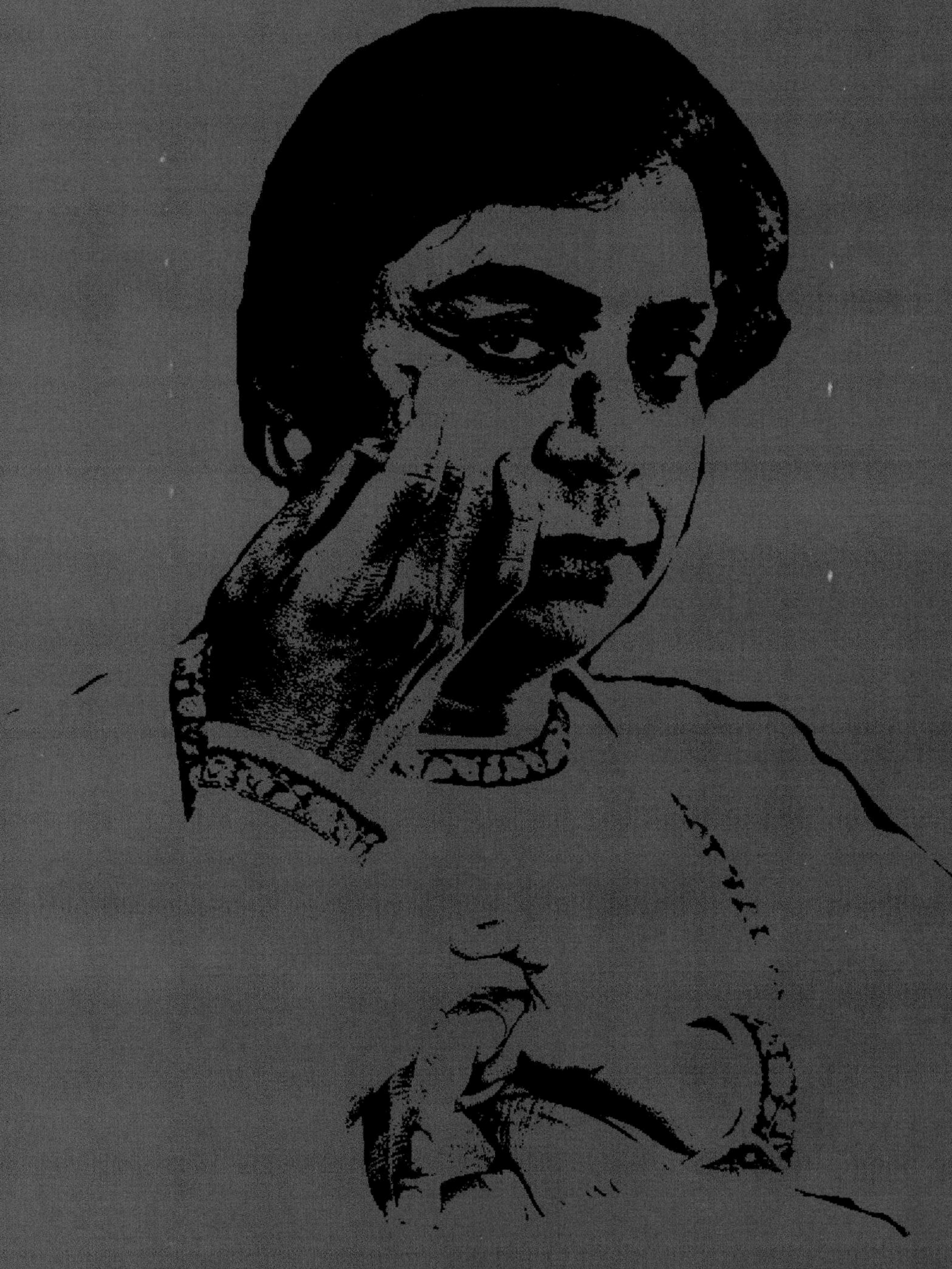

GENEALOGICAL TREE OF LUCKNOW GHARANA OF KATHAK

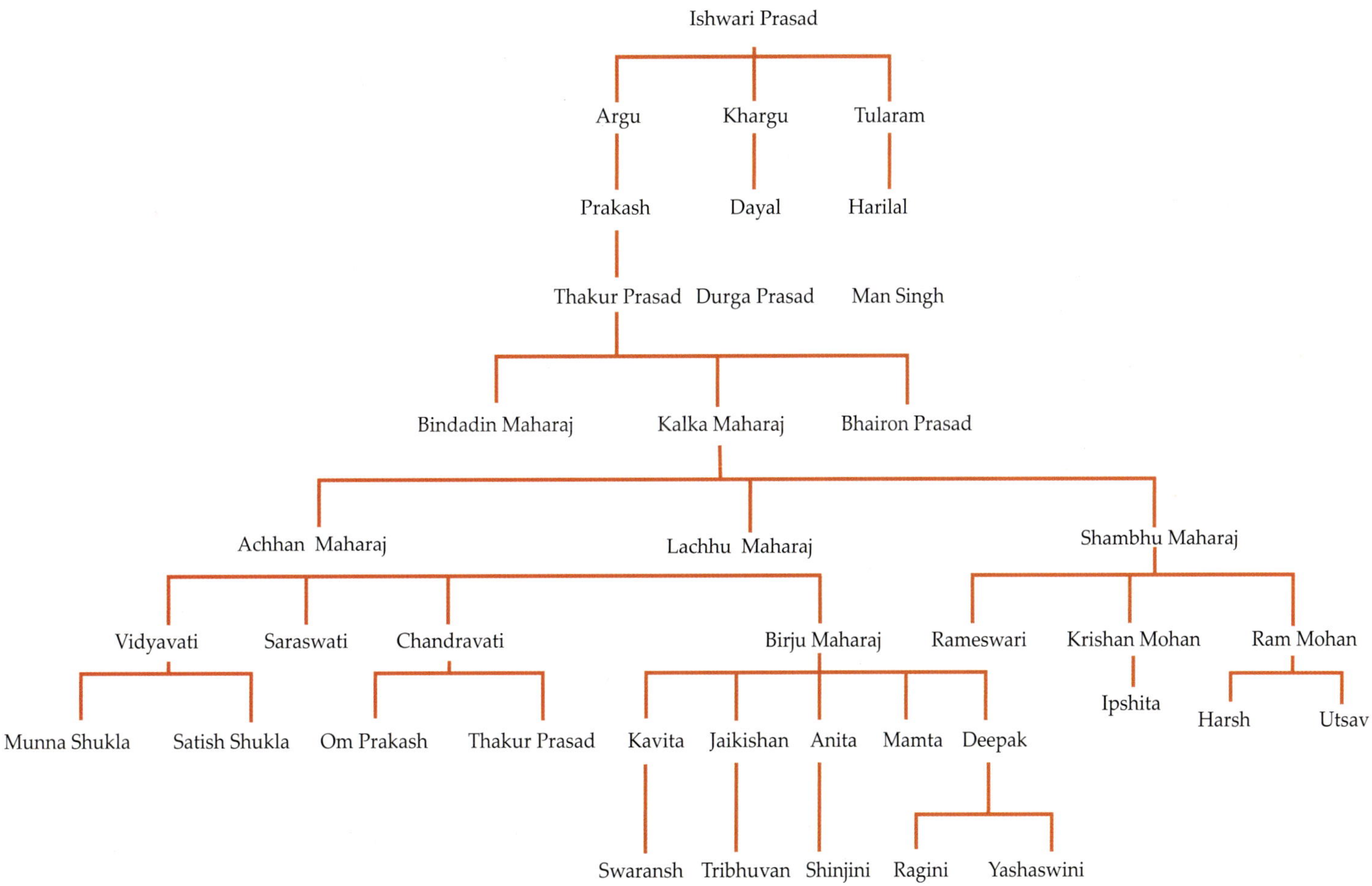

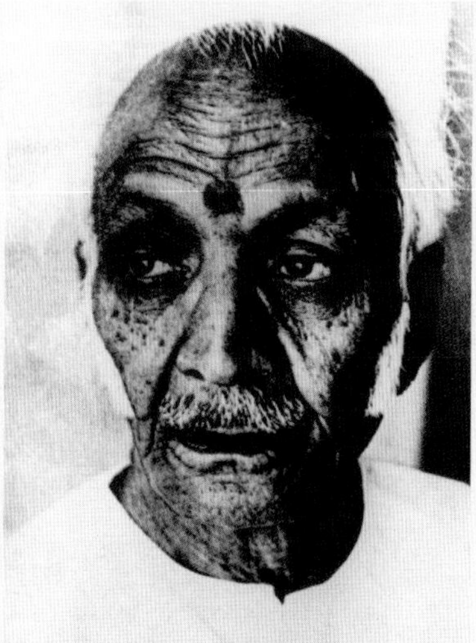

Facing page: A portrait of Durga Prasad, Birju Maharaj's great grandfather.
Above: Clockwise from top left: Bindadin Maharaj, Kalka Maharaj, Achhan Maharaj, Lachhu Maharaj and Shambhu Maharaj.

Mahadei, Birju Maharaj's mother.
Photograph courtesy: Prabha Marathe

Birju Maharaj's ancestral house in Lucknow.

Clockwise from top left: Lachhu Maharaj portraying Lord Krishna; Shambhu Maharaj; Birju Maharaj with his mother.

Above: In the Bhairavi Temple in Lucknow. Below: Annapoorna Devi, his wife.

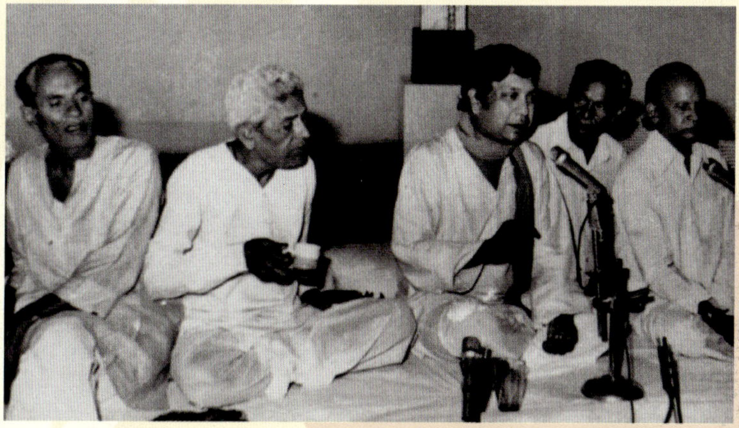

Clockwise from above: With senior masters from the Raigarh durbar; Dayaram and Mahadei; Admiring a painting of his father's dance pose; Sharing a light moment with Mahadei and Vikram Singh.

Above: Bindadin Maharaj's dance dress.
Below: Saswati in a traditional dance costume and headgear.

A performance in the seventies.

Above: With his aunt and mother.
Right: Dancing in the sixties.

A scintillating performance.

With Tirath Ajmani, his senior disciple. Photograph courtesy: Tirath Ajmani

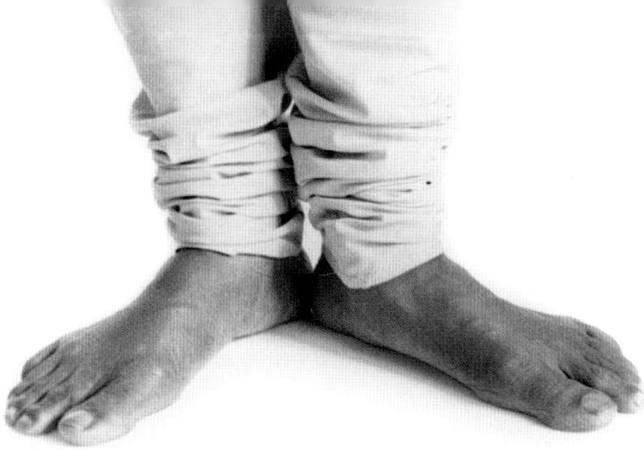

EARLY DAYS

With the untimely death of Achhan Maharaj, over were the days of childhood fun and frolic, kites, cinemas and so on. The only priority for Maharajji now was to look for work, to earn money. It had become difficult to meet their everyday needs and his mother Ammaji was extremely concerned about his career and wellbeing. She escorted him to all possible places where there was scope for meaningful work and a respectable income. They stayed in Kanpur for four-and-a-half years with the support of Maharajji's eldest sister, Vidyavatiji, and he studied privately with the help of Sitaram Baglaji, an older friend. Baglaji used to teach him English while Maharajji taught him dance.

Maharajji took up two dance tuitions of twenty-five rupees each. Often he walked long distances and requested passersby to help him cross the graveyard as he was afraid to do so alone. At times his mother skipped meals as there was not enough for both and when he asked her she would say she was fine in order not to bother the child. There were days when they slept almost half-starved. As for school, it was proving to be a big luxury for Maharajji. There was a decision by the Education Board to make vocal and instrumental music two separate subjects at the Intermediate level. At this stage Ammaji forced him to clear his school-leaving exams. When the results were declared, he excelled in both vocal and tabla. However, owing to his poor performance in English, he failed miserably on the whole.

When Maharajji was about twelve years old, he and his mother travelled to Nepal to participate in the celebrations of the marriage of the King's nephew. Those were times when travel was not easy. Several other artists also joined them in the hope that their works would be rewarded handsomely. Pandit Hanuman Prasadji, Pandit Kishan Maharajji, Tara Deviji (Sitaraji's sister) and Shri Hari Shankarji were among them. They walked for days and nights on foot, crossing several mountains—Chandragarhi, Sisagarhi, Ekdanta and Dodanta—stopping in tents for a few hours at night. They hired a stove and a small kerosene lamp as Ammaji usually cooked *khichdi* (a simple rice, lentil and vegetable preparation). It was a life of struggle and determination that finally led to Maharajji dancing in the royal courts as well as for the women in the interiors of the palace. They loved his dance and he managed to collect a fair amount of money as well as gifts from this trip.

Around the age of thirteen, Maharajji, along with his mother, his Sutto Jeeya and brother-in-law, went to stay with his uncle, Lachhu Maharajji, in Mumbai. They lived with him for less than a year in Dadar. It was here that Maharajji learnt from his uncle the intricacies of his lyrical style. His uncle also arranged for private tuition for him in English, though it certainly was not his favourite subject. The lady who came to teach him became helpless as he wrote dance *bol*s (rhythmic words) in place of his homework.

During his stay in Mumbai, Maharajji also enjoyed meeting cinema artists such as Madhubala, Meena Kumari, Jeevan, Sheikh Mukhtar, Motilal, Dilip Kumar, Ashok Kumar and Kishore Kumar. Once, Maharajji was listening to a music recording at Bombay Talkies with his uncle, when he saw a young man rehearsing some lines in the adjoining room. He found this rather funny as the man was repeating the words very fast and was acting weird. Ashok Kumar suddenly appeared and introduced the man as Kishore, his younger brother. That was probably the legendary Kishore Kumarji's earliest auditions with Shri SK Ojha. Even though Mumbai was good fun, the search for a proper means of earning a livelihood was bothering Maharajji.

Around 1953, Kapila Vatsyayanji, who had learnt under Achhan Maharajji and remembered young Birju, called him to Delhi to work at Sangeet Bharati—the same place where his father had taught. The job was a temporary one as he had been taken on a trial basis. The young boy was extremely excited and promised to work hard to prove his talent; it was a big boon but very challenging for him.

Along with Ammaji, they rented a small *barsati* (attic room) in Daryaganj from where he commuted by bus. Later they moved to Minto Road Railway Quarters, then stayed at Raja Bazar for a while and finally shifted to a place near Hanuman Mandir. From here he walked to school at five every morning. Maharajji had his first coffee at Madras Hotel, where one of the waiters was his favourite as he showed an interest in playing the tabla. Maharajji narrates how he once was in a hurry and forgot to carry his wallet, which he realised after drinking his coffee. He felt awkward, so he made a quick plan. He removed his jacket and threw it over his shoulders, stooped a little, squinted his eyes and made a weird face. Then slowly he moved out of the room limping on his left leg. No one really noticed. The next morning he went to the cash counter almost imitating himself from the previous day and paid the money.

Every morning, on reaching the school, Maharajji would enter the small room which stored several musical instruments. Without putting any lights on, he did his *riyaz* for about four to five hours until his sweat formed a pool on the floor, making it slippery. He would then sit down to rest as he picked up an instrument and tried his hand at it. His passion to learn helped him to understand the basics of several instruments and within no time he was comfortable playing the tabla, sitar and flute. Many times Maharajji would request the tabla artist, Lokmanji, to teach him some *bol*s but the latter would jokingly say that he did not want to lose his job! Maharajji, out of sheer determination, kept practising until one day he offered to accompany a senior musician, a sitarist. The audience was spellbound at Maharajji's skill with his untrained fingers. Having enjoyed success with the tabla, the young master started training himself on the sitar. Soon Lokmanji was no match for the speed at which he could play the instrument. All this joy in learning gave him more confidence. Maharajji recollects how this developed in his later days, when he had the great fortune of sometimes playing the tabla with Pandit Ravi Shankarji as he did *riyaz* in the late fifties at Lalaji's House near Ferozeshah Road.

Also later, during the early sixties, he used to tour with Aminuddin Dagar Sahib. Maharajji enjoyed accompanying him on the flute while Dagar Sahib sang compositions during train journeys or wherever they stayed in hotel rooms. He taught for four-and-a-half years at Sangeet Bharati. Among his students were Rani Karna, Malti Bhalla, Usha Gupta and Shakti Bhatnagar.

The young Birju.

Performing in the early sixties.

Dancing in front of a temple in Mathura.

Dancing to a bhajan (devotional song) *written by his grandfather.*

Above: With Lachhu Maharaj, Rohini Bhate and other friends.
Left: With Munna Shukla and Vijay Shankar.

*Above: Dancing with Pandit Kishan Maharaj on the tabla.
Left, from L to R: Rachna Sarang, Pandit Kishan Maharaj, a tabla artist, Hridyanath Mangeshkar, Birju Maharaj and Sitara Devi.*

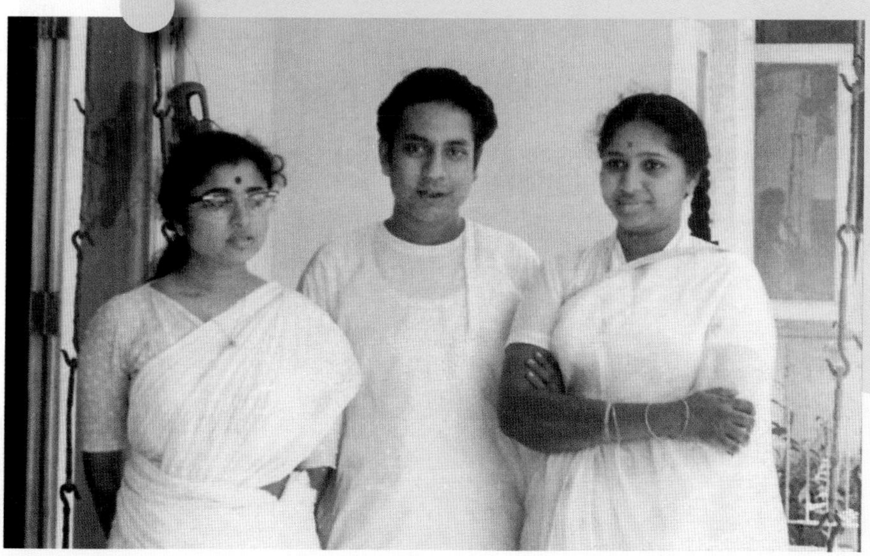

Above: An ornamental pose.
Left: With Usha Mangeshkar (on his right) and Asha Bhonsle.

Dancing at a gathering in Kolkata.

Above: With Shirley and Joseph, dancers from the USA.
Below: In conversation with Asha Parekh.

A pose from his famous composition, Maakhan Chori.

Depicting Lord Rama.

A dance recital in the early sixties.

A ghungat *(veil) posture.*

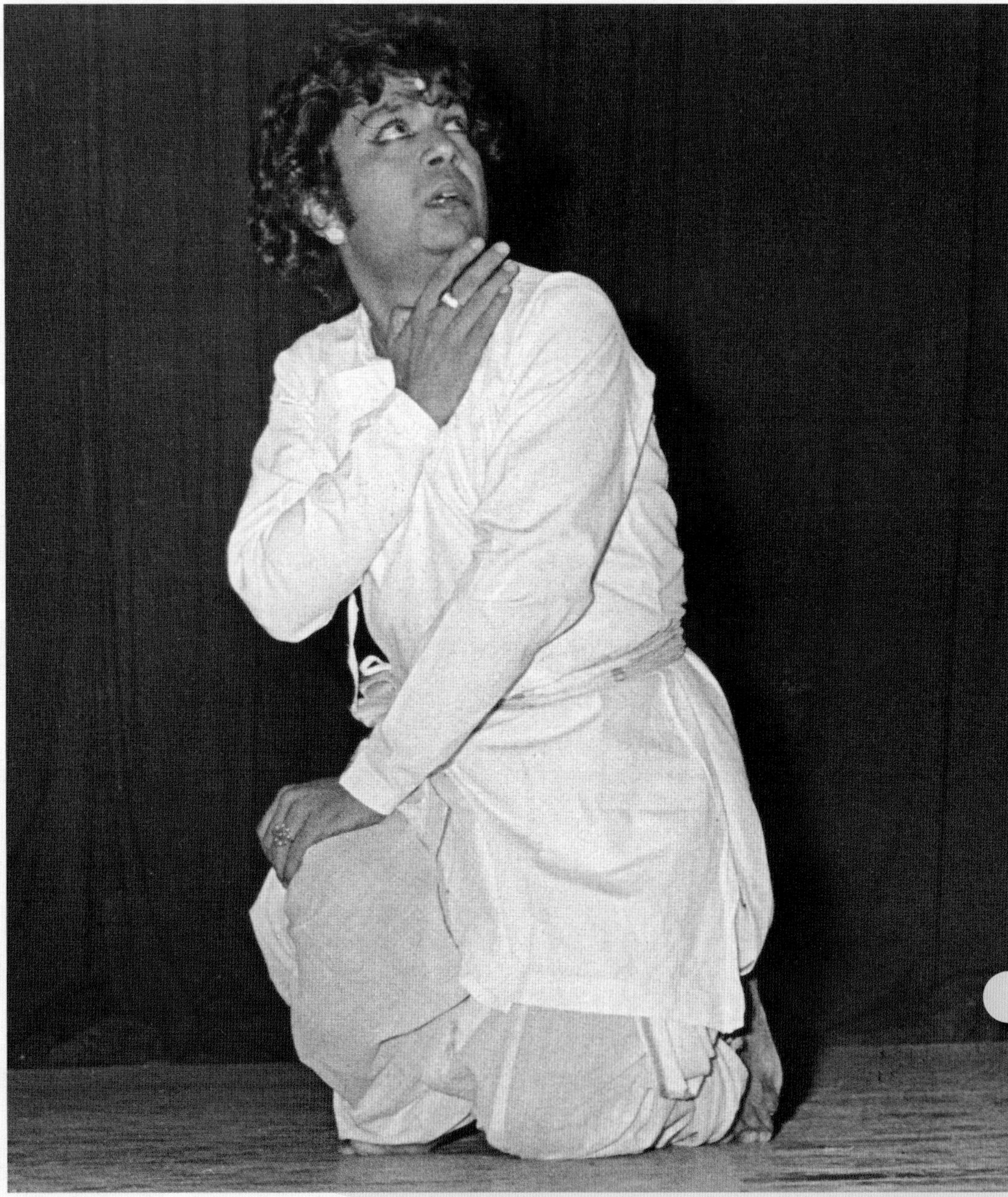

An intense expression while dancing to a Bindadin Maharaj bhajan.

A typical Kathak pose.

Depicting a vibrant mood.

DEVELOPING THE DANCE MOULD

At the age of nineteen or twenty, Birju Maharajji was invited by Shrimati Nirmala Joshi to work at Bharatiya Kala Kendra where Shambhu Maharajji had already joined. Maharajji's main task was to assist his uncle and also to compose items, ballets and dance-dramas for their new unit. Most of his students were small children, the only older one being Rashmi Jain (now Bajpayi). Maharajji taught Rashmiji with great care and sincerity so as to be able to win the minds of all the seniors. The first recipient of a Ministry scholarship who chose to learn from him was Pratap Pawar. Pratapji was nearly Maharajji's age and had been trained in Bharatnatyam. He became his first *ganda-bandh shagird* (formal disciple).

Maharajji took up the challenge of moulding his body for Kathak with a disciplined technique. His first task was to create a grammar for understanding every movement. For similes, he used nature and everyday situations. Everyone was quite curious when they heard about this new style of teaching and composing. Maharajji was actually enjoying his own thought process. Kathak was mainly practised as a solo form and experiments in thematic compositions and group choreography started only around the sixties. Kathak dancers, in those days, focussed on rhythmic interplay, speed and beauty of movements. The body was given very little importance. Even *abhinaya,* which was the origin of the dance and main communicative media, became secondary. The general masses recognised Kathak as a dance of *chakkar*s (spins) and *tatkar* (footwork) only, while some criticised it as a *makkhi-maar* (fly-batting) dance. The presentation of thematic compositions, beautiful choreographic lines and melodious accompanying music to enhance the mood had to be meticulously worked out. Dance-dramas, ballets and short items were composed; the masses liked it. During the sixties and seventies this was the most popular way of reaching out to the uninitiated audience.

Maharajji choreographed several successful dance-dramas during his tenure at Bharatiya Kala Kendra including *Kumar Sambhav, Shan-e-Avadh, Malti Madhav, Dalia* and *Krishnayan*. The first group compositions that he made were *Govardhan Leela* and *Holi Leela*. For *Holi Leela* Sitara Deviji was invited from Mumbai to play Radha (particularly to draw an audience, as she was quite popular in those days through her films) and Maharajji enacted the role of Krishna. No one had much experience on presentation, choreography, costumes or stage décor. However, they were full of ambition and commitment and their technique was strong. Sitara Deviji arrived on the morning of the show, as she had been very busy with her stage performances and film shootings until then. When the rehearsal began it was evident that she was not able to co-ordinate with the other dancers who had been practising for a long time. So Maharajji and her co-dancers had to prompt her throughout the show. Maharajji recounts how the whole experience was hilarious! The concept of proper rehearsals for choreographic work was obviously not well understood in those days and it was felt that the presence of mature dancers would make all the difference.

I was lucky to have seen the *Govardhan Leela* composition as a little girl, though I did not know Maharajji then. As a versatile artist, he was always inclined towards composing music. In some of the earlier dance-dramas the senior Dagar brothers (Fahimuddinji and Aminuddinji) composed the music, but later Maharajji did so himself. At times he also wrote the lyrics. During the preparation of the dance-dramas, Maharajji recollects with nostalgia how they worked through the night on every aspect of the presentation—painting, making of the sets, props, erecting them on the stage, as well as using all kinds of crude gadgets for creative lighting and sound effects.

The first major ballet composition, with the guidance of Lacchu Maharajji, was *Malti Madhav* in 1959. Krishna Kumarji played Madhav, Kumudini Lakhiaji was Malti and Maharajji was Makarund. Though he was not in the lead role, he felt happy as there was a lot of dance for him in comparison to the hero, who only had to pine for his beloved. Then came *Shan-e-Avadh*, based on the artistic life of Nawab Wajid Ali Shah of Lucknow. Maharajji portrayed the character of his illustrious great-grandfather Thakur Prasadji who was in the court of the Nawab. His dance, based on a dhrupad composition, *Kunjan Me Racho Raas*, by Dagar Sahib, drew tremendous applause from the audience. Soon after this, Kalidasa's *Kumar Sambhava* was prepared with a huge cast. The music was composed by the Dagar Brothers. Maharajji and Kumudiniji paired as Kamadev and Rati. This duet became immortal, as the two artists complemented each other perfectly.

Another interesting pastime that Maharajji indulged in was *kathputli* or puppeteering. Rehiji was a puppeteer at Bharatiya Kala Kendra and Maharajji composed the background music for many of his puppet shows. He also sang songs and spoke the dialogues for them. All the senior artists enjoyed working behind the scenes and Maharajji remembers some hilarious incidents during the recording of these productions. Once they were recording music for the ballet *Jhansi ki Rani* and during the war scene they needed the sound of guns. Toy guns with cork and small fireworks were being used. While inspecting one of these toy guns, John Lobo got burnt; he had a big scar on his cheek. On another occasion, Dagar Sahib was requested to speak some dialogues in the background for the play *Dhola Maru*. As they were listening to the recording before the opening of the show, Dagar Sahib was very upset on hearing the voice of a junior artist, Batukda

(Jyotirindra Moitra) in the role of the emperor, scolding him. Dagar Sahib commanded Rehiji to erase his voice. However, when everyone explained the situation, the matter got sorted out.

In another incident, Maharajji narrates his experience when he danced with his uncle, Shambhu Maharajji. Bharatiya Kala Kendra had arranged their duet at the Constitution Club in Delhi. Maharajji was about twenty or twenty-one years old and was very excited as well as tense. In the major part of the duet Maharajji performed *tukda*s (pieces of a composition) and *paran*s (types of rhythm) while Shambhu Maharajji complemented them with his mesmerising *gat*s, which were as much or at times even more powerful. Maharajji's close friends and associates at Bharatiya Kala Kendra were Keshav Kothariji and Kumudini Lakhiaji, who were scholarship-holder students under Shambhu Maharajji. Besides them were Maya Raoji and her sister Chitraji, Bela Arnabji and Gyan Madnaniji. Later came Tirath Ajmani, Prabha Marathe, Pradeep Shanker, Munna Shukla and others.

Maharajji, Pradeepji, Pratapji and Tirathji became good friends as they were almost of the same age; their family bondage is still very strong. However, Pradeepji passed away some time back. For a long time, these three disciples—along with Bharti Gupta, Uma Sharma and Rashmi Bajpeyi—were the most promising artists of the Ballet Unit, as it was called. They were the pivots of the Kathak Wing of Bharatiya Kala Kendra. Together they toured India and nearly half the world. They played lead characters in almost all the dance-dramas choreographed by Maharajji. Some of the unmatched roles that they enacted were Pradeepji as Dashrath, Kewat and Ravan in *Katha Raghunath Ki*; Pratapji as Kansa and Kaliya in *Krishnayan*; Tirathji as Shah Suja in Tagore's *Daliya*; Bhartiji as Radha in *Krishnayan*, Begum in *Shan-e-Avadh* and Tinni in *Daliya*; Umaji as Yashodha in *Krishnayan* and Rashmiji as Radha in *Shan-e-Avadh*.

I started participating in Maharajji's productions as a little girl with my first recital in *Krishnayan*. Then I joined the senior dancers in *Shan-e-Avadh* and *Kumar Sambhav*. My batchmates who also took part in the productions while we were still in Bharatiya Kala Kendra were Rekha Patki, Shraddha Dhabade, Krishan Mohan (son of Shambhu Maharajji), Ram Lakhan Yadav, Madhurita and Rachna Sarang. Later,

Subhash Dixit, Om Prakash Misra and Shivji Misra joined in the scholarship scheme. It was a great batch with a lot of healthy competition among us.

Maharajji recalls the time at Bharatiya Kala Kendra when the staging of the dance-drama *Malti Madhav* was to take place. He had to perform the role of two characters—Makarand and Aghore Ghant—as the artist playing Aghore Ghant had fallen ill. Maharajji of course knew the piece well and danced with élan, but at the end there was a fight sequence where Aghore Ghant was supposed to die on stage. As Maharajji fell down, he realised that the dancers had left behind *thali*s (plates) with beautifully lit candles. The stage, therefore, was not dark even after the lights had faded. Maharajji lay still for sometime but finally had to exit for his next act. He did not realise that every move of his could be seen as he crawled towards the wings. The audience broke into laughter and Maharajji felt terribly humiliated.

Another time, the troupe was presenting *Kumar Sambhav* at Ujjain. In the middle of the climax scene, an old man from among the organisers entered the stage, dragging a mike behind him and started singing the National Anthem. The audience stood up and the dance and music had to be stopped midway. Pratap Pawarji, who was acting the role of Kartik, was ready to pounce on the man, but Maharajji signalled him to keep his cool.

At Bharatiya Kala Kendra, Maharajji gained a lot of experience in producing dance-dramas, some of which became very popular. He then joined Sangeet Natak Akademi and took over the reins of Kathak Kendra, which had been running as the Kathak wing of Bharatiya Kala Kendra. The initial period was devoted to strengthening the organisation through its training programme. A proper syllabus had to be drafted, the period of training defined, types of training courses and programmes structured and so on. Maharajji was engaged in two positions—as a guru and as a choreographer. In the morning he conducted classes for the scholarship students and professional courses and in the afternoon he worked on the various choreographies. In the evening he took special classes for those senior students who could not attend classes in the morning; I was one such student. Maharajji really enjoyed teaching this evening session, as we had a good and sincere batch in our class. The next group comprised Neelima Azeem, Pallavi Bhagwati, Komal Dhameja and my sister, Vaswati. Another group was made up of Durga Arya, Malti Rawat, Jayshree Acharya, Bipul Chandra Das, Kalyani Pal and Veronique Azan.

Kathak was beoming popular and Maharajji had plans to make it still more elegant and beautiful. Almost every day he woke up with new ideas on how to make the students enjoy the inner meaning of abstract rhythmic compositions, the joy of playing with numbers and transcribing them into an imaginative body language. I am extremely lucky to have had the privilege of witnessing the development of this process. Initially it started with numerical phrases, which represented certain shapes or configurations. He later worked with syllables, which created images through sound/mnemonic variations as well as rhythmic combinations. According to Maharajji, the source of inspiration was his father who had composed some numerical *tihai*s (a cadence form) when he was in the court of Rajgarh Maharaj, and his uncle Lachhu Maharajji, who had visualised the famous composition, *Dha Ta Ka Thhunga,* in the playfulness of Krishna and Radha. He also recollects that he had heard stories of his great ancestors who had created rhythmic phrases to imitate the sound of moving trains, a gun cannon, horses galloping and so on.

Later, in the early eighties, Maharajji added another dimension to this playful yet educative way of teaching little children. He broke up the bigger rhythmic compositions into small phrases and used simple words, which create similar aural reflections so that the little ones find it easy to grasp and remember. For example: *Tata thhei, tathei, ta, tathieta, subzi, poori aur kachauri.* This immediately caught the interest of the young minds and learning was a joy for them. Maharajji created nearly a dozen *tihai*s of various rhythmic combinations of phrases. Since these had simple meanings, the children learnt expressions alongside. Maharajji developed this idea in order to nurture an interest and understanding among the general audience as well. He created *tihai*s to suggest movements in animals and birds, different types of games, moods and mannerisms, designs and diagrams. This has become a very successful way of reaching the minds of the general uninitiated audience and has inspired several musicians who have found this medium of rhythmic communication extremely effective. With this concept and understanding, Maharajji created some extremely successful choreographies such as *Laya Parikrama,* which suggests rhythms in every activity in the world; *Yati Darshan* (geometric patterns formed through rhythmic phrases) and *Tihai Roop* (visuals formed through the aural senses).

Maharajji was asked to compose a piece in honour of the delegates during the Asian Games held in Delhi in 1982. He decided to choreograph something related to sports and prepared *Nritta Keli* with twenty-four dancers. When he spoke about his ideas on the subject I wondered how he would structure each game through the rhythm and movement of dance. The compositions turned out to be amazing and Kabaddi, Kho-Kho, Tug-of-War and other games were experienced in an entirely new dimension of Kathak. This was perhaps the beginning of a new interpretation of rhythmic patterns and mnemonic phrases. The audience loved it as this was the most appropriate and creative way of uniting dance and games.

Maharajji's work in the eighties—*Naad Gunjan, Yati Darshan, Laya Parikrama* and *Sampadana*—opened the path for many young choreographers and helped them to develop contemporary ideas while maintaining the traditional richness of Kathak. At the request of Kona Prabhakar Rao (former Governor of Maharashtra), four senior gurus of classical dance forms came together to create a production. Guru Kelucharan Mohapatra (Odissi), Guru Vempati Chinna Satyam (Kuchipudi), Guru Kalyan Sundaram Pillai (Bharatnatyam) and Maharajji worked together on a common dance-drama (*Krishna Parijatam*) and some other short compositions. The seniormost Odissi dancer, Sanyukta Panigrahi, was selected to play Rukmini; Bharatnatyam dancer, Vani Ganapathy, was chosen for the role of Krishna, Shashikala in Kuchipudi was Narada and I played Satyabhama.

The script for *Krishna Parijatam* given by Vempatiji was in Telugu and every day I spent long hours trying to understand the meaning of each word from him. Maharajji mainly handled the closing item. The gurus worked with a lot of understanding and respect for each other. The programme was a tremendous success and I became famous in Hyderabad, as the character of Satyabhama has always been special in Andhra Pradesh and has been played by many leading artists. Our ex-Prime Minister, PV Narasimha Rao, affectionately called me his dancer-daughter after seeing this programme. We later presented *Krishna Parijatam* at the Chowdiah Memorial Hall in Bengaluru.

Around the early nineties, Prabhakar Rao again inspired Maharajji to compose another interesting piece on national integration, based on the famous song *Janani Janmabhoomishcha*. The choreography was staged at Vigyan Bhavan, Delhi, and then produced on television. Maharajji used dancers with typical adornments to portray nearly eighteen couples representing the different states of India while expressing different feelings of the song through typical body movements and gestures.

During the golden jubilee celebrations of India's Independence, Maharajji had choreographed a dance-drama, *Vande Mataram*. It portrayed the freedom movement and we had a lot of fun enacting the different freedom revolutionaries, imitating their postures, walk and mannerisms through the language of dance.

Showing how the body is streamlined in Kathak. Photograph: Avinash Pasricha

Facing page: With Kumudini Lakhia in Rati-Kamdev pose. Photograph courtesy: Kumudini Lakhia
Above: Kumudini Lakhia, dancing.
Left: Saswati in a joyful moment.

Left: Caught in a trance.
Below: During a rehearsal.

With Saswati in the mid-seventies.
Photograph: Avinash Pasricha

Right: Busy choreographing.
Below: Meticulously working on the finer points of a presentation.

Portraying Lord Krishna.
Photograph: Avinash Pasricha

Above: Reviewing a performance. Right: During a seminar at Kathak Kendra. L to R: Rohini Bhatia, Jeevan Pani, Keshav Kothari, Birju Maharaj, Munna Shukla and Rajendra Gangani.

Above: Teaching his children, Mamta, Deepak and Jaikishan, at home. Left: Saswati conducting a workshop.

A scene from Kathak Yatra. Photograph courtesy: Dinesh Poddar

Performances by Kalashram students, Saswati and others.
Photographs: Ashwani Chopra

Lost in the world of bhav.

Above: With Saswati at Gulab Bari in Kolkata.
Left: With his cousins Ram Mohan and Krishan Mohan.
Photograph: Avinash Pasricha

An expressive posture by Saswati.

A special duet with Saswati.
Photograph: Avinash Pasricha

The young Saswati in a dramatic pose.
Photograph: Avinash Pasricha

Expressing different feelings through body movements and gestures.

Facing page: In a reflective mood.
Above: Striking an emotional pose.

Moving ahead, as depicted in this dance posture!

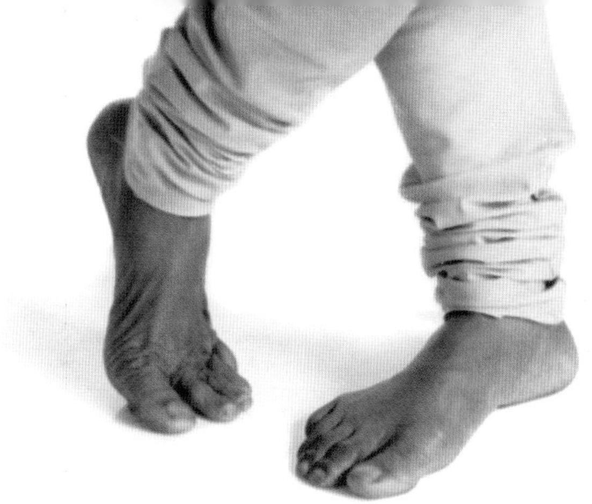

SPREADING WINGS

When he turned fourteen, Maharajji had two of his most memorable performances. The first was at the All Bengal Music Conference (Kolkata) where he performed a historic solo at Mahajati Sadan with Shri Nanku Maharaj (Bengal Tiger) on the tabla, another senior tabla artist and a pakhawaj player. Music lovers who could not enter the auditorium sat on the floor outside just to hear the rhythmic sound and enjoy the excitement. Word of this event spread fast and soon Maharajji made another major mark at the Sur Singar Sansad, held at Mumbai in 1955, at the invitation of Brij Narainji. Both these programmes were pivots of success in his career and people talked about them for months.

During this time Maharajji also performed in Allahabad, Kanpur, Nagpur, Bihar and the surrounding areas. He remembers an incident when he went to Motihari for a performance. The organisers had probably never seen a good Kathak artist earlier and had, therefore, assigned a small slot for him. But Maharajji's performance made such a stunning impact that he was requested to perform again the next day. However, he was scheduled for another performance in Kanpur. The next morning, as he was preparing to leave the hotel, he saw two or three *pahalwan*s (strong men) with big moustaches who warned him of the consequences if he left. Finally, Maharajji stayed back and performed another time, much to the delight of the audience.

When he was about eighteen years old, Chachaji and Ammaji called Maharajji to Lucknow on the pretext of holding his *janeu* (sacred thread) ceremony but they had actually arranged his marriage to Annapoorna Devi, the eldest daughter of Shrichandji, a senior vocalist from Varanasi. Though it came as a complete surprise, Maharajji obeyed his elders and tied the nuptial knot. He blushes as he remembers that he performed at his own wedding at the request of guests and friends.

Around the early sixties, Pandit Birju Maharaj, as he came to be known, received invitations to dance from several places in India including the South. He took his first flight to Chennai from Kolkata via Nagpur. It was a small aircraft and Maharajji was extremely nervous. He was throwing up and felt very uncomfortable all through the flight. At Nagpur he met Pandit Ravi Shankarji and was overjoyed to see someone he knew, hoping that the two would be in the same flight right up to Chennai. However, the latter was proceeding to Kolkata. The second leg of the journey was even worse, as it was a night flight and they were carrying onions in the aircraft, which emitted a terrible odour. By the time Maharajji landed in Chennai he was exhausted and sick; his ears were completely blocked. He was to perform within a few hours but he could not hear anything. For nearly half-an-hour he danced only by seeing Pandit Kishan Maharajji's finger movements on the tabla.

It was around this time that Maharajji stayed at the house of the legendary dancer Shrimati Balasaraswati in Chennai for nearly twenty-five days. Bala Amma, as she was known, had a deep affection and admiration for him. He had a few dance performances during that period and each time he returned home she would receive him at the doorstep with *aarti* (ritual of worship). Ranga and Viswa, her brothers and her daughter, Laxmi, all became his good friends and remained so till the end of their lives. Maharajji also learnt a *tillana* (rhythmic musical piece in Carnatic music) from Bala Amma and sang for one of her concerts. Many times they had informal sessions of music in her house at night when they shared each other's art and creativity with mutual admiration.

Maharajji also conducted some lecture-demonstrations in Chennai along with Pandit Kishan Maharaj, Viswa and Ranga. He toured Bengaluru, Mysore, Davangere and many other places with Maya Rao and Chitraji. Once Pandit Samta Prasadji was to play with him in Chennai for a concert but could not make it; the Sangeet Natak Akademi decided to send Mauji Ramji instead. Maharajji started trying out some pieces with him but found it very difficult and, in desperation, decided to quickly record his own tabla beats so that he would be able to perform with joy. The whole afternoon was spent in doing so. In the evening, when he started performing with the tape, he realised that he had not noted the compositions and had played extempore. Also, the *avartan*s (rhythmic cycles) left in between were asymmetric. Thus it was a real challenge to match the dance with pre-recorded music. Maharajji admits humbly that it was like learning one lesson after another and part of gathering great experiences in life. It was around this time that Maharajji also spent a lot of time in Kolkata and enriched his knowledge of music by listening to great master musicians.

Once, while performing for the Jalandhar Relief Fund programme, senior percussionists Iswaranji, Chaturlalji and some others went for an ensemble. One night they came to Maharajji and, out of curiosity, wanted to test his command over rhythm (though they had mutual admiration for each other). They asked Maharajji if he could recite a rhythmic composition that would hold good in four different *taal*s running simultaneously or, in other words, finish on the common *sama* (first beat of a time cycle) of four *taal*s (*teental, jhaptal, dhamar* and *ektaal*). Maharajji felt he had got trapped as if in a *chakravyuha* (labyrinth). However, he was determined to save his image and that of his ancestors and hence took up the challenge. For several minutes he kept reciting *bol*s extempore, groping and swimming in the world of rhythmic phrases. At times he felt he was about to reach the end point but then realised it was not complete. Finally, he silently prayed and recited a long *tihai* (a polyrhythmic technique used in Indian classical music) and reached the point of finish for all the four *taal*s. The four artists were overwhelmed. They carried him on their shoulders and paraded him in the balcony of the hotel, shouting cheerfully. That night, a grateful Maharajji prayed to his father and remembered his seniors with pride and respect.

It was probably around the same time that Kumudini Lakhia and Rajnikantji (her husband) saw Maharajji perform at Cowasji Jehangir Hall in Mumbai for the first time. She had earlier seen him as a playful boy in Lucknow, when she had gone there to learn dance under Achhan Maharajji. Kumudini narrates jokingly how during the programme Maharajji wore a white costume against a white background and only his head, palms and feet were visible. However, his dance left a lasting impression.

For nearly a decade, between the age of twenty-five and thirty-five, Maharajji was invited to perform in many places across India. He narrates a string of interesting incidents about this period. A memorable performance at Birla Matushri in Mumbai ended on an emotional note with a *bhajan*, *Pragate Brij Nandalal* and no one stirred, clapped or uttered a word. The audience, the musicians and Maharajji himself were as if in a trance. Then, after almost a minute, the audience burst into applause as if suddenly regaining consciousness. They encored for five to six minutes. It was a mesmerising experience.

Another time, in the Rampur exhibition ground, after ending a breathtaking *layakari* (rhythmic interplay) in footwork, Maharajji suddenly felt awkward as there was a hushed giggle initially from the audience and then from the musician's end. He blushed and was confused at such a reaction till one of the musicians pointed behind him to a stray dog standing right there and wagging his tail. Adding a little further to this humour, Maharajji sportingly bowed at him and accepted his appreciation.

Once while performing at the Sadarang Music Conference in Kolkata, he ended a fast *paran* (composition) with spins and suddenly there was a deafening sound. For a while the audience was shocked and then realised that a huge halogen bulb had exploded, probably from the drops of Maharajji's perspiration. There were tiny pieces of glass strewn all over the stage, but surprisingly Maharajji was completely unhurt. He stood still while they swept the floor for him to start again.

During yet another performance, the stage had a beautiful foreground with a waterbed lined with lilies. Maharajji was doing a long dance piece where he was moving upfront in some fast spins. As he finished he reached the edge of the stage and almost fell into the water. The audience stood anxiously to see him balancing on one foot; it was just enough to save him from falling. Later, when his friends asked him what would have happened if he had fallen, Maharajji said that he would have started the dance of Kaliya Daman, which shows underwater fighting between Krishna and Kaliya, the serpent king.

After his father's demise, there were several hurdles that Maharajji had to face in his artistic journey. In the forties and fifties classical dance was not so popular among the masses. In fact, even in the early sixties, when I began my dance career, none of my friends could relate to my love of Kathak. The present generation is lucky that the hard work of the masters of the sixties and seventies helped to develop the presentation of Kathak and slowly motivate the common man to understand and appreciate its subtle nuances.

Maharajji was just twenty-one or twenty-two years old when he was invited to dance in Jhansi. His uncle Lachhu Maharajji went with him. There were other artists invited as well. When Maharajji was doing his make-up, he could hear some restless, rowdy people among the audience hooting and disturbing the artists who were performing on stage. He was really nervous and wanted to quit, but his uncle gave him moral support, some quiet advice, and encouraged him to go on stage and start his performance. Soon after he began, he could hear loud whispers and people gossiping. Maharajji stopped abruptly and announced that he would do a new piece, which he had especially composed depicting the brave queen Laxmibai of Jhansi. The audience welcomed this with great enthusiasm. Through his dance movements and *abhinaya,* woven with interesting rhythmic patterns, he portrayed the courage and valour of the immortal queen—how she fought and defeated her enemies. The audience was amazed and reacted with thunderous applause. There were screams of 'encore' and Maharajji obliged them by doing the piece again and then again. They loved it.

Maharajji then showed them some of his other dance numbers and went back to his composition, *Jhansi ki Rani*. The magic worked and he managed to hold the audience spellbound for nearly one-and-a-half hours.

Once, while performing at the Meerut Nauchandi *mela* (fair), he again felt some disturbance among the audience. Maharajji tried hard to engage them, but they were least interested and just wanted some light entertainment and folk music.

In the late seventies Maharajji accepted another invitation to perform in Mumbai. After his recital, there was to be an entertainment show by film stars. The audience became so rowdy and uncontrollable that Maharajji refused to dance and the organiser had a tough time managing the situation. The famous character actor Jairaj stepped in and spoke to the viewers but nothing really improved. Maharajji promised never to accept such invitations as he was hurt by the disrespect shown to such a divine art.

I, too, was witness to a couple of such situations with Maharajji. Once we were invited by Spic Macay to perform at a college in Kota. As I finished the invocatory number and started my dance, the students began talking and making a noise. Maharajji then stepped on stage and very softly and peacefully appealed to the students to listen for just fifteen to twenty minutes, as the programme had been arranged with the intent of sharing the beauty of art. Maharajji then danced for nearly one-and-a-half hours. The students were so moved that after the performance they all apologised for their bad behaviour.

Between the seventies and eighties Maharajji had suddenly put on some weight. He had a pot belly and a fluffy face. Even though his dance was beautiful he had to hear criticism about his physique. The Asia Society Director from the USA had come to see the troupe's performance and to book them for a long tour. When she saw Maharajji she initially rejected him owing to his big stomach. However, after seeing his performance, they included him; but Maharajji prayed for a better physique every day.

He also wanted to be innovative and bring in new elements into the Kathak dance form. Once when he was in Kolkata and was to perform at Kala Mandir, he met Chetna Jalan and her son Sachetan, and invited them to his performance. Young Sachetan was unwilling to come, but Maharajji promised him something special if he showed up that evening. Half-way through the performance Maharajji called his sons Deepak and Jaikishan and his cousin Krishan Mohan on stage. He suddenly stopped the music and asked those on stage to keep the major beats and breaks of the *taal* going on their instruments and through clapping. Maharajji himself started reciting some syllables, randomly criss-crossing the patterns in several symmetric and asymmetric phrases. The sound effect thus created was tremendous, somewhat like rap music, which was fairly unknown in India those days. It had the desired effect on the audience as well as on Sachetan. At the end of the show he expressed his joy and gratefulness to Maharajji for having opened a door for the appreciation and understanding of rhythm in Kathak.

Some years ago, Maharajji and I went for a programme to Mumbai. When we reached the venue, Priyadarshini Park, we saw a huge crowd of youngsters enjoying Zakir Hussain's tabla performance along with his percussion band. Some people were actually jumping and dancing with the drummers. Maharajji was a little apprehensive and uncomfortable with the mood that was building up. However, when he finally went on stage and started his invocatory number, quite a few people were still in an excitable mood and were walking around. He then started to speak in a warm tone and demonstrated the depth and subtlety of the rhythmic phrases. The soothing effect of the accompanying *ghungroo*s (bells worn by classical dancers) was magical. The audience sat in rapt attention. The programme went on for over two hours and Maharajji and Zakir Bhai were in ecstasy, sharing and creating every minute. After the performance hundreds of young people wanted their autographs and photographs; some even expressed their ignorance about the richness of classical music. When we returned, Maharajji advised me to check on the type of crowd and atmosphere before accepting an invitation to a programme.

More recently, Arindam Choudhury (economist and management guru) had invited Maharajji to talk to a group of MBA students in order to inspire and educate them in the understanding of classical music. Maharajji was initially hesitant but then accepted it as a challenge to stir uninitiated minds. After a general lecture-demonstration on Kathak and North Indian music, he invited the students to ask questions and seek clarifications, if required. One boy said that he could seldom appreciate pure classical music as he never understood the meanings or feelings of the *raga*s (a combination of notes sung or played at different times of the day or night) and the *swara*s (solfa notes) and that there was no visual created, so he switched off the radio on classical music. After thinking for a few seconds, Maharajji told him to concentrate for a while with his eyes shut and started singing the *alaap* (prelude to the main musical composition) in Rag Saarang. Then Maharajji sang the same notes with some meaningful words that were simple and easy to understand. The boy opened his eyes and exclaimed, 'Wow, what a different experience; the same notes became alive and meaningful.' Maharajji advised him to always try and imagine words in the place of musical phrases, according to whatever the mind reflects. It was a completely new approach to music even for me. Maharajji had managed to explain difficult rhythms and melodic structures by giving easy examples and similes, which anyone and everyone could understand and enjoy.

Just as in everyone's life and career, Maharajji's career has seen several ups and downs. Sangeet Natak Akademi had organised a festival at Red Fort; it was a magnificent programme attended by a huge crowd. The artists were top of the line—Ustad Amir Khan Sahib, Pandit Bhimsen Joshi and Maharajji. Everyone was in a great mood and gave some memorable performances. This was one of my earliest experiences of the greatness of Maharajji and I started seeing the aura around him.

At Sri Krishna Gana Sabha, Chennai, the year when Maharajji was awarded the Birudu-Nrithya Choodamani, his performance was attended by great stalwarts such as the late Bala Saraswati, Lalgudi Jairaman and others. It was a magnificent presentation and the audience gave him a standing ovation. The Sabha was so pleased with this response that they immediately confirmed his date for the following year. The next morning Maharajji conducted a lecture-demonstration at the Sabha's Natya Kala Conference. Dancers of different genres attended it and were greatly inspired by his elegant style. Maharajji also shared the stage with other great artists in duet presentations.

He performed with Girija Deviji in Kolkata, Delhi and Mumbai quite a few times. The wonderful rapport between them and the warm cordial feeling they shared added to the grace of the performance. With the late Shobha Gurtu, he did *bhav* presentations in Kolkata and Mumbai. Both enjoyed sharing the music, lyrics and expressions with each other. Then he did several very interesting programmes with Pandit Kishan Maharaj, Pandit Rajan and Sajan Misra in India as well as in England. People enjoyed these, as there were elements of impromptu rhythmic challenges that only great masters can handle.

Shaw Wallace had organised a festival, Antiquity, in Kolkata. The venue was a stage built in front of the Victoria Memorial Museum. Seven great maestros of different classical dance forms, Kelucharan Mohapatra (Odissi), Vempati Chinna Satyam (Kuchipudi), Bipin Singh (Manipuri), Kalyan Sundaram Pillai (Bharatnatyam), Govindan Kutti (Kathakali), Kalamandalam Kshemavathy (Mohiniattam) and Maharajji performed short solos as well as some pieces together. In the morning they decided on what these pieces would be, but there was not much time to discuss the last *abhinaya* in detail. When that number started, no one really knew what was to be done. Maharajji recollects how, in this last expressive piece, poor little Krishna was indefinitely being shoved from one artist to the other and finally playfully thrown up in the air with no one to catch him. In a flash of common reaction, both Maharajji and Kelucharanji stepped forward to hold the baby and cradle him to sleep. There were few other moments of uncertainty, which were understood by the sensitive audience. They laughed their guts out at the simplicity of these great men.

Among these joint programmes, the most memorable and divine was a duet presentation by Maharajji with Kelucharanji at Delhi's Kamani Auditorium. It was organised by Kalashram for the Vasantotsava festival. Both the masters had shared some presentations earlier in Mumbai, Kolkata and Delhi but this one was absolutely divine. The perfect chemistry they shared on stage and their mutual admiration brought heaven and earth together. Maharajji's *abhinaya* as Krishna and Kelucharanji's as Radha were so sensitively portrayed that the audience could almost feel the divine couple dancing in Vrindavan to enchant each other.

Maharajji's programmes have always been special and mesmerising for me and his fans. When I saw him perform at devotional places, it was as if he was possessed and beyond anyone's reach even after the performance. In Nathdwara, within the precincts of the temple, as he danced in the presence of the deity, Sreenathji, we could almost see the Divine Lord in him. When he played Krishna, he was transformed totally. The *mahant* (main priest) and a chosen group of the audience witnessed his performance with disbelief.

At Pandharpur, I had the great fortune of dancing with him for his composition, *Abhishek of Lord Vithal*. We had to bathe and decorate the deity and that put me in a trance, so much so that during the evening performance, both Maharajji and I kept dancing extempore through the power of some supreme force. I truly enjoyed becoming a devotee in offering.

Some years ago, at Shirdi Sansthan in Nasik, inside the main temple of Sri Sai Baba, we presented compositions written and sung by Maharajji in praise of Baba. Tears of joy rolled down our faces as we all shared Maharajji's feelings for this great saint. At many other devotional places such as Tirupati in Andhra Pradesh, Gokarna in Karnataka, Ram Mandir in Nasik, Sankatmochan in Varanasi, Banke Bihari in Jaipur and the Iskon temples in Vrindavan and Bengaluru, I have seen the audience watch his dance as if mesmerised. At the end of the programme people rush to the stage just to touch his feet. I have heard elderly people say that they have seen the divine in him. Maharajji especially enjoys the comments from little children who innocently relate to the easy and playful pieces that he chooses to dance at times.

In 1961 Maharajji travelled abroad for the first time. He went to Karachi along with Bharti Gupta and Begum Akhtar and his tour was a great success. His first trip to the USA was in 1963, where he led a troupe sponsored by the Asia Society. This was his longest tour and stretched for nearly two-and-a-half months, covering the length and breadth of the vast country. Among the finest in the troupe was Ustad Amjad Ali Khan with whom Maharajji played the tabla in many concerts.

His next tour was to the USSR, where the Bharatiya Kala Kendra troupe of nearly thirty-six artists was invited by President Krushchev to present *Kumar Sambhava*. On the inaugural day of the show all the artists were asked to assemble in the lobby and board the bus as soon as it arrived, as parking was a problem. Everyone reached in time except Maharajji and Purushottam Dasji, the great pakhawaj artist. They had lost their way. Initially they could not find the correct lift as the hotel was huge and when they got into it Maharajji pressed the last button on the panel demarcating the floors. As they came out of the lift, both shrieked in amazement, fearing that they had arrived at a different hotel. They stepped in and out of the lift a few times and finally abandoned it, holding each other's hands out of fear. They crossed several unknown rooms—the saloon, laundry room and so on —and after a great deal of effort found someone who pointed to the steps going up. On climbing these they let out a sigh of relief when they saw the reception, lobby and other familiar areas. The lift had taken them to the basement and they were totally unaware of this. As if that was not enough, Purushottam Dasji told Maharajji that he needed *aata* (flour) for playing his pakhawaj. Maharajji looked around and found no one from their troupe and realised that it was already late. He tried to call the attendants at the hotel and helplessly cried out, '*aata*'!

'What *aata*?' came the response from the attendant.

Maharajji's knowledge of English did not go beyond 'yes', 'no', 'very good' and some other basics. However, in an effort to explain, he said, 'brad'.

'Bread?' asked the attendant.

'No, no brad,' said Maharajji again. He then made gestures of cutting in several pieces.

The attendant thought he wanted sliced bread. Maharajji then made gestures of smashing, crushing the bread, as if in a powdery heap.

The attendant asked, 'Flour?'

This came as a reverse blow, as Maharajji had only heard the word 'flower' and was confused, but nonetheless he nodded hesitantly. The man disappeared. In the distance, a faint sound of an annoying horn could be heard continuously, which they presumed was for them. Seconds seemed like ages and finally the man returned with a packet in hand. As if in great relief Maharajji opened it and found *maida* (refined flour) inside. Purushottam Dasji was unhappy as this was of no use to him, but Maharajji insisted that they should accept it as they had no choice. When they rushed to board the bus, they saw angry faces approaching them as they were really late. For the show that evening, Purushottam Dasji struggled all along trying to wet the *maida* and apply it on the drum, but it dried and fell off in no time. The scene in the wings was hilarious, as the sound kept fluctuating and Purushottam Dasji tried his best to keep tune. They laughed their lungs out after the show was over.

Those were tough times abroad when all kinds of problems with language and food, even on stage, proved very embarrassing for Maharajji. Once, during the same tour, he needed a big towel so Maharajji went to the maid in charge of his floor and tried to communicate this. He was unable to do so with words so he caught her wrist and signalled her to his room. She was quite reluctant, but as soon as he moved with her to the bathroom she yelled, '*Neeyat Neeyat*' (No, No). Maharajji quickly picked up a towel and started enacting his need for a big size wrap to wipe his body and tie around him. The maid laughed aloud and soon brought him a huge beach towel, which was perfect.

The troupe had to perform in Laos. Vietnam was at war and there was a lot of tension in that part of the world. Maharajji and the troupe, which included senior artists such as Uma Sharmaji, Pratap Pawarji, Bharti Guptaji and Tirath Ajmaniji, arrived at the airport and, much to their surprise, were asked to board a military aircraft. They were the only passengers on the flight. The seating arrangement was not the regular kind; there were two rows of bench-like seats along the windows facing each other and the luggage was piled up in the space between. There were no seat belts, tables or air hostesses. The plane took off with a jerk and just as it was in the air Umaji leaned back against a window which suddenly opened. A fierce wind gushed in and she was almost pulled out. Two of the artists jumped to her rescue and one caught hold of the string attached to the window in order to keep it closed. After a few minutes, a man showed up from the cockpit with a formal grin. Everyone screamed and began to tell him what had just happened. He took the string rather coolly and tightened it with a knot around a hinge and signalled with a thumbs-up that all was fine. Maharajji and the others were really upset and furious. Through the small windows they saw the aircraft flying quite low. As it approached the mountains, it felt as if the aircraft would crash and a less than two-hour flight was enough to make them vow not to accept the return trip on a military plane.

By the time they reached the venue it was already past the time announced for the show and the audience was waiting. Fortunately the programme went off well. The organisers promised not to send them back on the same flight and that came as a huge relief. Little did they know that something else was in store for them! On the return journey they were made to board the Red Cross Relief aircraft, which was meant for injured and deceased soldiers.

A few years later Maharajji and Kumudiniji were sent to Baghdad by the Indian Council for Cultural Relations (ICCR). Other senior artists on that trip included Pandit Ravi Shankarji and Ustad Allah Rakha Khan Sahib. Almost every day before and after the performance they all had to sing an anthem in praise of the ruler Abdul Karim Qasim. It was difficult to get vegetarian Indian food so most of the time they had to be satisfied with bread, butter and fruit. Maharajji remembers one evening when a huge party was thrown in honour of the visiting artists. There were tables that were miles long, laden with food, but nothing vegetarian. Finally they found a corner table with some fruit. However, other than grapes even the fruit was cut in beautiful designs with meat toppings. So they filled their stomachs with grapes.

A trip to Rangoon (Yangon) on the occasion of India's Independence Day celebrations was really eventful. A huge stage had been built in the middle of a lake and suddenly it started drizzling. Members of the audience pulled out their umbrellas, whistling in excitement. As they were getting late, Manika Prasadji, the tabla player, quickly removed his slippers and pushed them under the raised orchestra platform and Dev Shankarji (the vocalist) began to do the same, when he realised that the footwear was falling into the lake. They somehow held back their laughter and the show began. The soft drizzle made the instruments sound weird and the smooth linoleum spread on the stage became so slippery that both Maharajji and Kumudiniji could barely balance themselves through the spins and poses. The audience, however, just loved it. After the show they were invited for dinner at Prime Minister U Nu's residence. Both the musicians tried hard to hide their bare feet but it only became more obvious and most people were amused or stared in surprise.

They had one more performance to mark the celebration, which was held in the banquet hall of a hotel. The organisers had arranged for the performance to be along with the dinner. Kumudiniji was terribly annoyed with this. Additionally, a young girl had been invited to entertain the audience with some light dances in the beginning. Maharajji and Kumudiniji refused to perform, so finally they had to rearrange everything with more dignity and élan.

During a tour of the USA in 1962, through the Asia Society, Maharajji accompanied Ustad Amjad Aliji on the tabla in several concerts. He recollects a memorable programme in a huge arena theatre where the audience was seated all around. During the dance items Maharajji asked the group to dance, keeping in mind the audience seated on all sides; but for the sarod they decided to sit in a way so that half the audience saw Maharajji playing the tabla and the other half saw Ustadji with the sarod. This turned out to be a great hit.

In 1973, I had the privilege of going abroad with Maharajji's troupe for the first time. The tour was through ICCR and we went to the USSR and Czechoslovakia. Our Kathak group had nearly fourteen members. Begum Akhtar was there with her accompanists; also present were Deepali Nag (vocalist) and Prakash Vadehra (flutist). Our tour leader was Keshav Kothariji. We performed in nearly twelve cities and what an experience it was being up there on huge stages and some very old classic theatres! The only unpleasant fact was that most of the stages had rough uneven surfaces and our bare feet got hurt every day. After each performance, we sat at night to pull out small splinters of wood from each other's feet. Some of the stages also had a small slope and we really had to control our balance during the pirouettes and fast moves.

It was in Russia that I first experienced the strange effect of sunlight shining brightly past midnight. Only around three in the morning did it become a little dark and by 4:30am the sun was up again, bright as ever. None of us could sleep; so we had Maharajji and Hari Shankarji (the vocalist) sing for us almost through the night. Often we slept at 3am and woke up at 10am just in time to catch breakfast. We had the privilege of seeing a performance of the Bolshoi dancers; it was amazing, as if they were perfect dolls moving uniformly. Maharajji told us about their discipline in maintaining a perfect body and their practice sessions, old and young all working on the same floor. This was an inspiration for him, which strengthened his own teaching methodology. By this time Maharajji had realised that there was a great need to make his students and young performers understand the importance of aesthetic beauty in dance.

In 1974, Beate Gordon of the Asia Society came to Delhi to invite Maharajji on a two-month tour of the USA. He and Kumudiniji were to be the main dancers and I was chosen to share a couple of items with them. Though Mrs Gordon was initially hesitant on my selection, she was convinced that I was not a complete misfit. When I finally came to know about my going I could not sleep for several nights. Not even in my wildest dreams had I imagined that I would go to the US with such senior artists! The day I landed in New York I had to pinch myself to believe that I was not dreaming. However, the excitement in the days preceding the trip and the long journey with such a huge time difference threw me completely out of gear. We were invited to watch a show at the Carnegie Theatre on the first night of our arrival, but I was in a daze and fell asleep in the middle of the show, dreaming that I was the heroine of the ballet, *Romeo and Juliet*, which we were watching.

The first show at Carnegie Hall was a lifetime opportunity for me, I had to prove myself as a good dancer to match the standards of Maharajji and Kumudiniji. I was extremely nervous and did not want to let down Mrs Gordon. Before the show Maharajji came to me and, having sensed my tension, gave me some inspiring advice. He said I should only concentrate on and feel good about the qualities that I have—my speedy pirouettes, expressive eyes, fast movements and so on. He also told me that I had been selected by him among so many others and that should be a source of confidence and strength. This helped to calm me down and I went on to perform the most challenging dance—a duet—with Maharajji.

At the end of the show I was only waiting to see Mrs Gordon's expression; she came in with a gleaming face. After congratulating Maharajji and Kumudiniji, she turned around and hugged me, saying I had really lived up to her expectations. That night in my room I cried, laughed and prayed. We had a long two months' tour of numerous cities—we did programmes, lecture-demonstrations and workshops. I saw the two great artists perform with such elegance, especially in the beautiful Rati-Kamdev duo.

Maharajji's spontaneous improvisations in rhythm were well appreciated by the people who had no exposure to Kathak. Mrs Gordon lovingly called him 'Beerju'. Once she told him that his dance was so natural and non-pretentious, that she would be happy if he wore no formal costumes. So Maharajji started dancing in his *kurta*s and people loved him. In the lecture-demonstrations, Kumudiniji spoke so well, explaining the background and the development of Kathak. Several workshops were arranged in the universities and many young students enthusiastically joined them after witnessing our performances. We had performed in nearly all the major cities of the US—New York, Washington, Chicago, Boston, Pittsburg, Houston, Philadelphia, Madison, San Francisco, Los Angeles, Seattle and many more. It was indeed a very successful tour.

On our way back we had one performance in London arranged by Birendra Shankar of Sanskriti at the Queen Elizabeth Hall at South Bank. This was another terrific experience. Unlike America, London had a much larger Indian community even in those days. As soon as Maharajji stepped onstage there was a thunderous applause; people were waiting to see the magic of his dance and he danced right into their hearts.

I think it was the most fulfilling tour of my life as I had witnessed the most gorgeous places, theatres, museums and had enriched myself in the art of presentation both on stage as well as for the general public in schools and colleges. Since then, I have travelled with Maharajji almost all around the globe. Sometimes it is a large troupe of fourteen to fifteen members and at times we have just about seven to eight people including musicians. The smallest group was of six artists, which is rare.

In 2000, ICCR organised several tours abroad to celebrate the new millennium. We were sent to China with a troupe of eighteen members and our performances started on 1 January 2000. Never had we witnessed such cold weather; everything was freezing. The roads looked like a glass sheath; even to walk ten steps from the hotel to the bus stop was frightening. Most of us slipped once or twice. The cyclists fell every now and then and our sightseeing trips had to be cancelled. Visiting the Great Wall of China was also an experience—as soon as we got off the bus our shoes got stuck in the snow. We were shivering down to our bones.

Our programmes at Beijing and Guangzhou were very well received and on our way back we performed in Malaysia and Burma. Subsequently, we went on several interesting tours to the UK, USA, Canada, Holland, Germany, Trinidad and Australia.

During our visit to Malaysia in 2000, we were invited to visit the Temple of Fine Arts in Kuala Lumpur. Here we met Swami Shantanandaji. It was a wonderful meeting between the two great gurus, almost as though a divine chord had been struck. The following year Swamiji invited us to Perth for a workshop and some performances. Later, in 2004, he arranged a week-long celebration in Varanasi where Maharajji was seated on a throne-like pallanquin that was carried through the lanes going down to the Daswamedh Ghat on the Ganges. His disciples washed Maharajji's feet and took him on a huge dais erected on a big board floating in the river. Around twelve pandits chanted Vedic mantras and performed prayers, thereafter Maharajji was crowned the 'Kathak Nritya Chakravarty' amid thousands of onlookers. Dancers danced in his honour and it was truly a celestial sight. Later, Swamiji invited us to his other centres in Perth, Kuala Lumpur, Coimbatore and Singapore. Swamiji passed away in 2005, but the warmth, dedication and love that he embedded in his students towards art is alive even today.

In 2011, ICCR requested Maharajji to recompose *Ritu Samhara* with a new group of dancers.

Describing a typical hand gesture.

Photograph: Avinash Pasricha

Clockwise from above left: With his dance troupe in Italy; With Janaki, Kumudini and Saswati in New York; With his troupe and Allesio Alba (the host) in the Vatican City.

Clockwise from top left: With Hari Shankar and Gopal Chakravarty in the USSR; With Birendra Shankar (host) and Lakshmi Shankar in London; With Saswati on a beach in Cyprus.

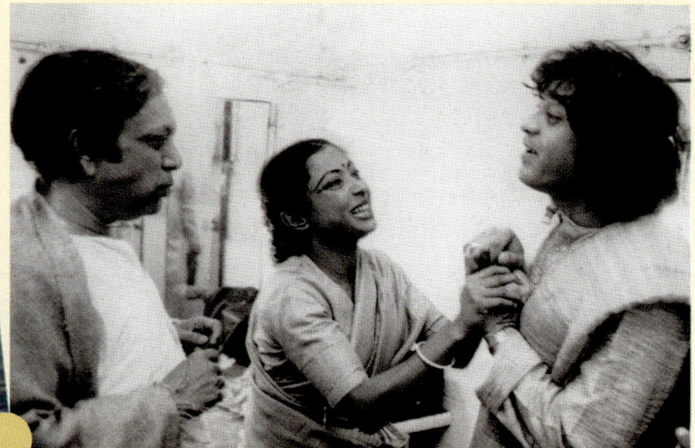

Clockwise from top left: With Saswati in Moscow; Sharing a joke with Saswati and Zakir Hussain after a performance; Saswati with flamenco and tap dancers; In Europe with Durga Arya and Dilip Acharya.

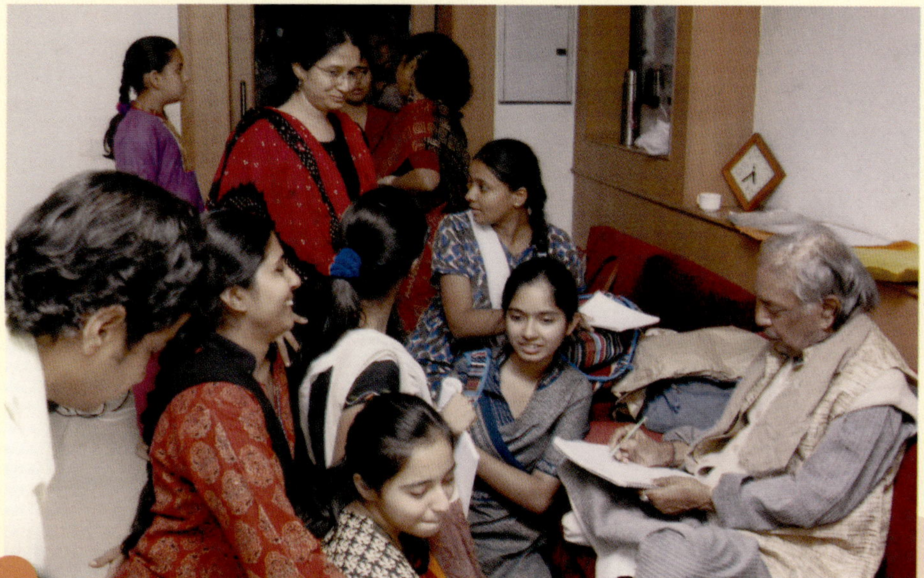

Clockwise from above: Correcting dance notations amid students; With Saswati in China; A jovial moment in Germany.

Thaat, *a static posture.*

Birju Maharaj performing a mother-and-child pose.

Above: The troupe enjoying a sunny day in Japan.
Left: With Kumudini Lakhia and Atul Desai in Germany.

Clockwise from above: *Birju Maharaj in a versatile posture; After a performance at the Avignon festival in France; With Latif Ahmad Khan.*

Clockwise from above: With Pupul Jayakar and former Prime Minister, PV Narasimha Rao, in Japan; At a flower show in China; Enjoying the snowfall in Vienna.

Above: Taking a bus ride across the US with Saswati.
Right: A typical finishing stance in Kathak. Photograph: Avinash Pasricha

Above: With friends after a vocal concert in New York.
Left: At Ali Akbar Khan's house in California.

Clockwise from left: At a performance in Thailand; At a vocal concert in Vancouver; Enjoying the company of friends in New York.

Clockwise from above: Birju Maharaj with two of his students from China, Shanu and Manu; Three generations of Kathak dancers in London—Akram Khan, Birju Maharaj and Pratap Pawar; In Washington with Ambassador Surendra Kumar, Sonal Mansingh and Mrs Kumar.

Above: Senior dancers at Kalashram—standing, L to R: Singhjit Singh, Charusija Mathur, Deepti Omchery, Birju Maharaj, Sadanam Balakrishna and Leela Omchery. Sitting, L to R: Prerna Shrimali, Leela Samson, Madhvi Mudgal, Swapna Sundari and Saswati. Left, L to R: Sukanya Shankar, Ravi Shankar, Birju Maharaj and Saswati.

A devotional pose. Photograph: Avinash Pasricha

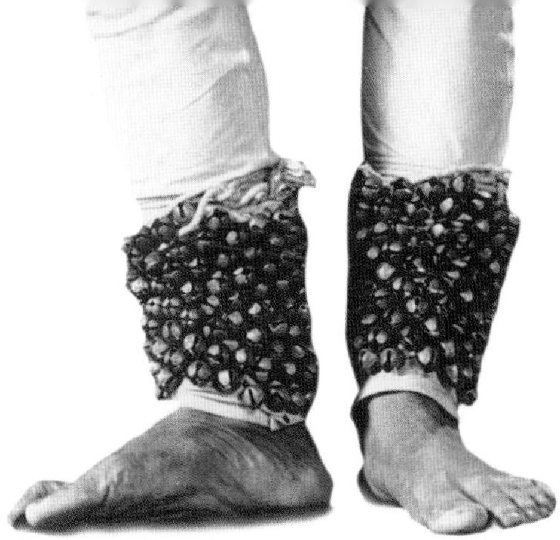

BEYOND KATHAK

In the sixties and seventies Lachhu Maharajji was a very successful dance-director in the Mumbai film industry. Some of his immortal works were *Mughal-e-Azam*, *Pakeeza* and *Teesri Kasam*. For *Mughal-e-Azam,* Maharajji was invited to dance along with Gopi Kishanji and Vyjayanthimala in the last royal court dance scene. Then somehow it changed to Maharajji and Gopi Kishanji. During the rehearsals Maharajji kept telling Gopi Kishanji to take smaller leaps, but during a final trial Maharajji jumped even higher. He really felt bad and humiliated and hence quit the assignment as he thought that he was having to compromise with his style for the sake of the film. However, during the premiere of *Mughal-e-Azam*, he performed a memorable solo on the sets of the famous Sheesh Mahal or Palace of Mirrors. He remembers the galaxy of stars in the audience, the lavish party with drinks flowing and also how elegantly Raj Kapoor made the announcements.

Maharajji was once invited to direct a dance piece for Vyjayanthimala in *Chhoti Si Mulaqat* but after a few days he called it off as he was not happy with it. Around 1971-72 Maharajji composed some dance pieces for Asha Parekh's stage productions—*Anarkali* and *Chaola Devi*. They worked hard and the result was very successful. He composed a special *tarana* for her, which he has refused to teach anyone else till date.

In 1976-77, Satyajit Ray, the legendary film-maker, was planning his Hindi film *Shatranj Ke Khilari* in which he recreated the era of Nawab Wajid Ali Shah's reign in Avadh. I was doing my graduation in Anthropology at the Delhi University at that time and usually attended my dance classes only in the evenings. Manikda (Satyajit Ray) saw a performance of mine at Vigyan Bhavan and requested Maharajji to choreograph two dance sequences for the film. Maharajji gladly agreed and after several discussions in various compositions by Bindadinji they selected one of his *thumri*s for a court dance sequence. The next step was to find a suitable dancer for this scene. Maharajji introduced Manikda to many of his students but ultimately I was selected. My parents had to be coaxed to give their permission. Manikda asked Maharajji to try and reproduce the style that prevailed in the courts during that time. Maharajji's ancestors, having served the Nawab for a long time, had left vivid images of their style in the family. Maharajji had also heard several stories from his mother and uncles.

Working on *Shatranj Ke Khilari* was such a memorable experience. It started with the recording of the music for the two dance sequences which Maharajji was choreographing. One was a group dance with Amjad Khan (as Wajid Ali Khan) who enacted the role of Krishna dancing with *sakhi*s (concubines). Two of Wajid Aliji's own compositions were used in this piece—*Hindola Jhoole Shyam* and *Jan-e-Aalam Rabas Mubarak*. The other was a solo number in a court scene. Bindadinji's Bhairavi, *Kanha mein tose haree*, was chosen, for which Maharajji sang the playback soulfully.

Maharajji did nearly twenty-five takes during the recording and was still not satisfied with his own song. Finally, Manikda called me and said, 'Creative *Manush konodin* satisfied *hobe na; onake bolo bhishan bhalo hocchhe*.' (A creative artist will always remain self-critical, tell him this time it has come off wonderfully.) So we all shouted 'encore' after the next recording and Maharajji finally felt good. Then came the preparation of the piece. I think there were three or four instances in my lifetime when Maharajji worked one-on-one with me. This film was one of them. I worked day and night on my body lines, gestures, stances, expressions and finally the result was beautiful. The viewers loved it and everyone still talks about it.

The shooting for the film was a unique experience. Manikda's team was like a family and we easily became a part of it. Maharajji and he shared a great relationship with mutual admiration. Maharajji wanted to compose a fast, exciting dance piece, but Manikda told him to try and recreate the ambience of the courts as he had heard and known. Maharajji then developed an even greater respect for the genius director and composed a lyrical, emotional and elegant dance piece, regal and appropriate for the film. During the sets we would see Manikda taking care of every minute detail. My head bowed at his feet when I saw him helping the most junior set boys as he took the hammer and nailed the frames and the curtains or arranged the carpets. During the lunch or tea breaks Maharajji, Manikda, Amjad Khan and I often sat together as Maharajji sang old compositions or recited some *bol*s. Amjad Khan had a great music sense and sang very well.

Maharajji also composed music for three dance *bhav* sequences for a film in Guyana (*Fields Of Sugarcane*), which were choreographed by Pratap Pawarji as he was a teacher there. Then, after a long gap, Maharajji's association with Madhuri Dixit during our visits to the USA brought him back to the film world in early 2000. He composed a short dance sequence for Madhuri in the film *Dil To Pagal Hai*. The background music was mostly based on drums and Madhuri excelled in the presentation. Her fast pace, perfect stance, body movements and hypnotic smile were enviously good.

Maharajji composed a group dance sequence on a *bandish—Aan Milo Sajna* sung by Pandit Ajay Chakrabarty and Begum Parveen Sultana for the film *Gadar* received wide appreciation. His choreography for *Devdas*, directed by Sanjay Leela Bhansali, was a masterpiece, keeping the classical Kathak style intact. Madhuri's mesmerising expressions and subtle moves, along with the elegant choreographic presentation by Maharajji's trained students, remain memorable. I had the opportunity to assist Maharajji in the film and it was a great experience to see the creativity and sincerity in the work of Sanjay Leela Bhansali, which reminded me of Manikda's meticulous planning of his films. Maharajji also did the choreography for the film *Pranali*, for the upcoming actress, Nargis Bagheri.

The next big project was Kamal Hassan's film *Vishwaroopam*, in Tamil and Hindi. Kamalji is another fantastic actor—very creative and sincere. He initially spent some time learning Kathak steps from Maharajji and then worked with total dedication for the choreography. For Maharajji, it was a challenging task to create movements and rhythmic patterns, which would be appropriate for a non-Kathak male dancer. The composition was, of course, extremely interesting.

Since childhood Maharajji had a great inclination towards music. He started composing music and ghazals at the age of twenty-one or twenty-two and trained young vocalists, Anjan Chatterjee, Dilraj Kaur and Suman Lata. The first songs that Maharajji composed were for Anima Das at the All India Radio. Initially he was hesitant and always told them not to mention his name publicly, but soon people were curious to know the name of the composer and he became quite popular.

A Shiva-Tandav pose. Photograph: Avinash Pasricha

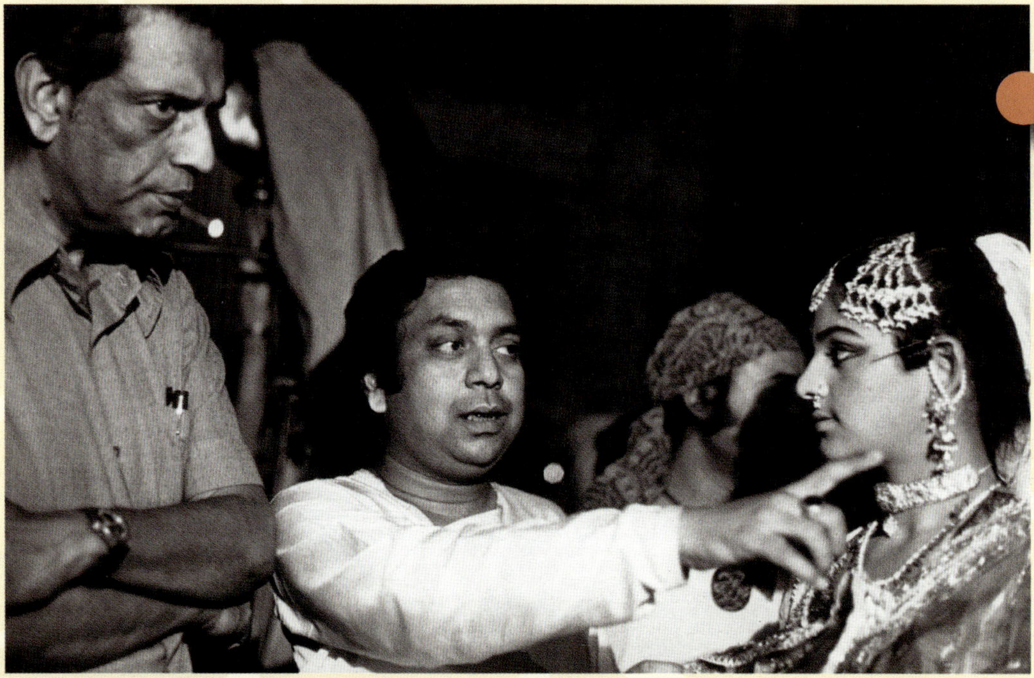

Above: On the sets of Shatranj Ke Khilari, *with Satyajit Ray and a student.*
Below: An abhinaya *pose with Shobha Gurtu's vocal rendering.*

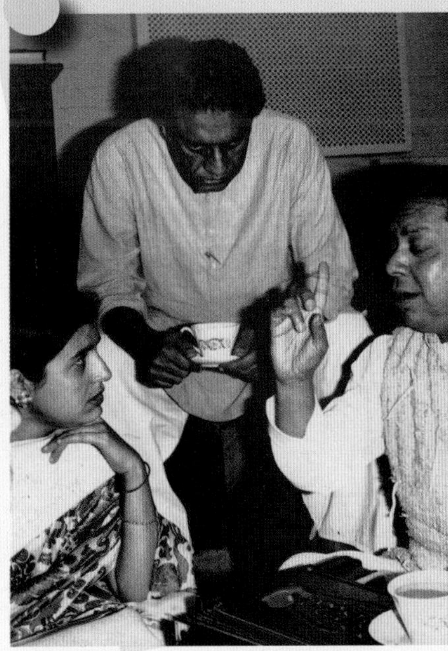

Clockwise from above: In conversation with Gopi Kishan and Lata Mangeshkar; During the recording of a song from Shatranj Ke Khilari*; At the recording studio with Satyajit Ray and Ruma Guha Thakurta.*

A scene from Shatranj Ke Khilari.

Above: Giving last-minute instructions to Saswati, on the sets of Shatranj Ke Khilari.
Left: Durga Lal on the pakhawaj and Birju Maharaj playing the tabla.

Left: Admiring Ravi Shankar's line drawing at the photo exhibition organised by Kalashram.

Photograph: Ashwani Chopra

Below: Playing his favourite drum, the Maharashtrian naal, *with Jumnabai in Pune.*

Clockwise from left: At a book release function with Shovna Narayan and SH Raza; Admiring his own work of art; Being felicitated by Amjad Ali Khan.

Facing page: Portraying Bindadin Maharaj.
Above: Ritu Samhara, *a production in six classical dance styles of India, choreographed by Birju Maharaj, performed in Korea.* Photograph courtesy: Dinesh Poddar

A touching performance in New Delhi with Kelucharan Mohapatra. Photograph: Avinash Pasricha

Clockwise from above: Performing with Ajay Chakravarty's vocal rendering; Playing jugal bandi*; An intense* abhinaya *with Kelucharan Mohapatra.*
Photograph: Avinash Pasricha

Playing the tabla with gusto.

And what a spectacular finish!

Directing Kamal Hassan and the troupe for the film Vishwaroopam.

Photograph courtesy: Kamal Hassan

Left: Performing abhinaya *with Rajan Misra's singing. Below: On the sets of* Devdas *with Jackie Shroff, Shah Rukh Khan, Madhuri Dixit and the dancers.*
Photograph courtesy: Sanjay Leela Bhansali

Deepak Maharaj as Romeo and Saswati as Juliet in the Shakespeare production.

Photograph: Avinash Pasricha

Right: The joy of achievement.
Below: A contemporary choreography by his disciple Vaswati Misra.
Photograph: Vicky Roy

A formidable stage presence.

THE DANCER DIVINE

Having been born into a family of artistic geniuses, it was to be expected that Maharajji would carry forward this rich legacy. But in all fairness it is believed that the *gharana* has reached its zenith with Maharajji's creative brilliance. There are very few people gifted with multiple artistic qualities but Maharajji is certainly one of them. An unmatched Kathak dancer, a superb vocalist, a generous teacher, an imaginative painter, a player of several musical instruments and an unassuming, simple human being—Pandit Birju Maharaj is an icon, a living legend.

Besides these creative qualities, the greatest gifts that Maharajji has given to the Kathak world are the aesthetic sensibility of beautifying the lines and body of a dancer and the interpretation of rhythmic phrases into meaningful statements with visual appeal. These have been greatly appreciated by the masses; the audience now shares a common thought process and an inner dialogue. Maharajji's rhythmic interpretations have also influenced musicians, especially percussionists. The beauty of lines and angles in a dancer's body was not given much importance in Kathak earlier; frozen poses at the end of each rhythmic piece were limited. Maharajji has created numerous beautiful stances to decorate the finishing point of the pieces, most of which have become very popular with young dancers today.

He has a clear vision and a complete understanding of the basic purpose of art. He does not believe in just the content and technique, but delves much below the layers. His creations and interpretations—both in the solo repertoire as well as group choreography—have a strong base and a subject. During a lecture-demonstration at an MBA institute, Maharajji inspired a young man to appreciate traditional classical music. The easiest way, according to him, is to imagine a visual meaning of whatever reflects from the notes of the *raga* and even imagine some words, if required.

Once Maharajji explained the *alaap-vistaar* of *raga*s to some young students and music lovers in simple words. He asked them to imagine the *alaap* as if it was something that appeared in a body with no adornments. Referring to *Raga Malkauns*, he saw it as if it was a freshly bathed body, lightly clad, with bare, strong shoulders, approaching elegantly in a slow gait and a regal smile. The artist then respectfully welcomes the *raga*, touching and washing its feet, seating it with honour. As the *taan*'s develop he decorates the *raga* with rich clothes, jewellery, headgear, beautiful drapes and perfumes. The majestic form of *Raga Malkauns* is then complete as the artist goes into *Drut Laya* and respectfully sees the *raga* off, only to await its arrival again soon. In the same way he referred to some other *raga*s, personifying them in different personalities, thus unfolding the character of each one separately.

I have been blessed with the privilege of seeing Maharajji—his performances, choreographies, lectures and thought process behind every aspect—since the early seventies. Kathak dancers until then were only conscious of their skill in the technique, particularly in rhythm, speedy movements and fast pirouettes. Much of the hand movements were repetitive and the finishing poses were all similar. It was Maharajji's creative mind that was always searching to make the style more elegant and lyrical. He thought about the entire body and the co-relation of different parts—the torso, limbs, neck and eyes. Each movement made a definite statement on its own, which he could see and analyse. Thus the technical aspects of his dance also became lyrical and poetic.

Maharajji's presence on stage bears such a divine form, with an aura around him, that no costume, adornment or make-up is required. As soon as he appears, the audience sees the divinity in him. His communicative powers are also magical. Seeing him perform Krishna episodes is like seeing the little god in him. Some of his most popular numbers are: *Gat Bhav—Makhan chori* and *Chand khilona; Mayur and Mahawat Gat; thumri*s—*Ghir ghir aayin badra, Balmare chunariya maike, Dhaaye gaho* and *Mohe chhero na Nand ke; bhajan*s—*Meri suno Nath jaise, Aise Ram hain dukhharan* and *Udhav mohe Brij bisarat naahin.* Other well-known compositions include *Dekho hori ke khelaiya, Bihar ko apne, Kaise ke jaun* and *Jhoolat Radhe.*

Some of his favourite rhyhmic patterns are *tihai*s with meaningful representations such as *chusta susta, telephone tihai, battakh chaal, horse galloping, imitating birds, skating* and *hockey*. The *taal*s that he likes the most are *teentaal* (sixteen beats) and *dhamar* (fourteen beats). He describes the nature of *taal*s in very interesting ways—sometimes referring to nature and animals and at other times comparing the *leheja* (mnemonic structure) of *taals* to the walk of different human beings. These references are so perfect that the students really enjoy their classes.

Maharajji's style is a blend of his father and uncles. His wrist movements are graceful and body movements dignified. His frisking feet positions and the preparation of the mood before each small piece are all influenced by his father, as are the spontaneous creations in the rhythm. Lachhu Maharajji's lyrical movements and soft body angles, extempore s*anchari* (simile) of expressions and delicate gait left an impressionable mark on Maharajji. Another very interesting aspect that inspired him was the imagination of various moods that his uncle demonstrated in rhythmic compositions. Shambhu Maharajji's style was most vigorous and masculine; his hand and body movements were very powerful and his footwork strong. He had extremely captivating eyes and his neck positions always made definite statements. Birju Maharajji's style has a lot of these qualities, particularly the sharp neckline angles and the eye expressions. Maharajji believes that all three have influenced his dance—Shambhu Maharajji's expressions and commanding personality, Lacchu Maharajji's graceful and lyrical body angles and his father's rhythmic genius—and all are precious gifts to treasure.

Besides his family—mother, father and both uncles—there are a few others who have left an impressionable mark on Maharajji's life and career. Some of them are dear friends who have inspired him to think and create beyond what he received as training from his ancestors. Prominent among them are Kumudini Lakhiaji, Keshav Kothariji, Jeevan Paniji and Gopal Dasji. As a student of Maharajji at Bharatiya Kala Kendra, Kumudiniji had known Maharajji when he was very young. She saw a great talent in him not only as the torchbearer of his family beholding the richness of the *gharana*, but also as a trendsetter in his style and presentation. She used to motivate and challenge him to surpass the popular global icons of dance of those days. She also helped him to understand the importance of costumes, make-up, stage mannerisms and to bring in more aesthetics. Maharajji obeyed her like a little boy.

During the late fifties, Keshav Kothariji came to learn for some time under Shambhu Maharajji in Delhi and there he became friendly with Maharajji. They lived together in a small room on the mezzanine floor above a garage at 5 B, Pusa Road. Classes were held on the ground floor of this house. They cooked, ate and slept together, thus sharing their views on dance. Keshav Kothariji advised Maharajji on presentation, the selection of items and programming. Later in the eighties, when Keshav Kothariji became Director of Kathak Kendra, he motivated Maharajji to choreograph some of the most abstract innovations. *Laya Parikrama* was the first one performed at AIFACS theatre. Thereafter Maharajji choreographed *Ang Tarang, Ghungroo Sangeet* and many more.

Gopal Dasji met Maharajji in the seventies when he became Director of Kathak Kendra. He was a literary person and very disciplined. During this association, Maharajji came to know about the work of many famous writers and poets and he composed dance pieces on these. At Kathak Kendra, Maharajji directed some very successful dance-dramas and group choreographies—the most popular ones being *Katha Raghunath Ki, Hori Dhoom Macho Ri* and *Roopmati Bazbahadur.*

Jeevan Paniji came in as Director at Kathak Kendra. He was from Orissa and had a profound knowledge of Indian art and heritage. Having been in Sangeet Natak Akademi, he had travelled extensively all over India and interacted with dancers, musicians, painters and art scholars. Among his numerous qualities and interests was his passion for reading. Thus, as he took charge of Kathak Kendra, he made it a point to educate himself as much as possible about the details of the dance form. His modesty and simplicity immediately struck a perfect note with Maharajji. Both had great admiration and respect for each other and enjoyed sharing their knowledge and ideas. I was lucky that they had a lot of confidence in me and were proud of my work and dedication. Thus I was soon a part of their discussions on programming and presentations. It was a great learning process for me as I shared my wild thoughts with them, which they heard patiently. My artistic career grew in leaps and bounds under the guidance of these two great mentors. Jeevanda inspired me to imagine new creations, both in my solo and choreographic work. During his time, Maharajji created some extremely innovative and successful choreographies—*Anamya Loha, Yati Darshan, Sampadana, Samachar Darpan* and *Naad Gunjan*. Jeevanda's sudden demise was a terrible blow to both of us; Maharajji was in a state of depresssion for quite some time.

Some of the other people who hold a soft corner in his heart are Reba Vidyarthy (dance teacher and like a sister to Maharajji), Purushottam Dasji (pakhawaj maestro), Mohammad Jan Sahib (sarangi player), Gopal Chakraborty (sitar player), Vijay Kumar (painter), Anuradha Hui (dancer), Hari Kishan Behera (Odissi guru) and of course, his three favourite disciples—Pradeep Shanker, Pratap Pawar and Tirath Ajmani—with whom he spent a good part of his youthful days.

Behind the powerful artist—Pandit Birju Maharaj—dwells a soft, compassionate human being. Like most of the seniors in his family, he is ever willing to help anyone who is in need. Those students in whom he has seen a commitment and passion for art have been helped by him to overcome financial problems, family differences, health-related matters, mental tension, social stigmas and so on. I have seen some incidents that have left a deep impression on me. Once, as we were returning from a trip to Rajasthan, we got off at the Old Delhi railway station near the small meter gauge platform. The *coolie* picked up our luggage and was following us; suddenly someone uttered softly, 'Birju! Birju!' Maharajji turned around and within seconds screamed in excitement, 'Kanhaiya!' Maharajji rushed towards the *coolie*, took away the bags and hugged him tight. Both friends cheered with joy, recollecting the lost days of childhood. As I watched this affectionate reunion, tears rolled down my eyes.

Ammaji told us that they had once gone to Dalman and when they got off at the station, there were no *coolie*s. Maharajji asked a passenger to help him put the big tin trunk and bedding on his head and, without any hesitation, carried it out. Another time, Maharajji was coming to my house on Minto Road when a cart-puller was struggling with his cart, which was full of spare parts. Maharajji parked his car, a Morris Minor, and pushed the cart with the man till it climbed the ascending road; the man thanked him profusely and uttered blessings.

Maharjji has always said, 'Blessings and good wishes are the biggest treasure of any person, no gifts or money can match these words of love.' Perhaps because he had to shoulder huge responsibilities after his father's death, Maharajji missed his childhood and still craves for it. His heart is still like that of a child; he loves to play with toys and enjoys the company of children. Kids feel extremely comfortable and happy learning from him. Seldom have I seen great artists of such stature interact with all age groups, all levels of learners; in fact, he takes it as a challenge to teach weak students. Besides his artistic work, Maharajji's fascination is electronic gadgets. He loves to buy all kinds of small or big electronic items for audio, video, recording or games. His cupboards are full of gadgets, cords, wires, batteries, screwdrivers, torches and more. He tells us that as a young boy he sometimes thought that if the family profession was not his responsibility, he would have been happy to have become a motor mechanic.

Maharajji's modesty and sense of responsibility was noticeable right from his teenage days. Having lost his father early, Maharajji knew that he had to handle his career, his life and family as best as he could. When his middle sister, Saraswatiji, passed away, leaving behind five daughters, Ammaji decided to keep them in Lucknow under her care and guidance. Maharajji loved them dearly and they saw in him both their parents. As they grew older, Maharajji got them married.

Among his nephews, Munna Ṣhuklaji is the oldest; he is the elder son of Maharajji's eldest sister, Vidyavatiji. Since he was just six to seven years younger than Maharajji, much of their childhood days were spent together; both shared a lovely bond. Munnajji received the National Scholarship from the Ministry of Culture and took training under Maharajji. He was very good in *taal-laya* and Maharajji enjoyed sharing some of the intricacies of the rhythm of the Lucknow *gharana* with him. After his training, Maharajji helped him to establish himself as a guru at Kala Chhaya, Pune and later brought him back to teach at the Kathak Kendra in Delhi.

During my tenure as a student under Maharajji, his uncle Shambhu Maharajji died of cancer, leaving behind two sons—Krishan Mohan, sixteen and Ram Mohan, ten. Maharajji taught them both with love and care. Later, his second nephew, Om Prakash Misra, the elder son of his youngest sister, Chandravatiji, came to stay with them and learn from Maharajji. His sincerity and talent helped him to become a guru at Prayag Sangeet Samiti in Allahabad initially and then a professor at Benaras Hindu University.

Among Maharajji's own children, Kavita, his eldest daughter, was very talented. As a little girl, she played the role of the child Krishna beautifully. Maharajji felt that she was the one to have truly imbibed his style. Unfortunately, as she grew older and got married, she stopped dancing formally, owing to the family tradition.

All his children have an inborn gift of art and he happily imparted his training to groom them as successful dancers. His second daughter, Anita, took up painting and sculpture as her profession and has carved a prominent place for herself in Delhi. Jai Kishan, Mamta and Deepak have continued with the family tradition and are successfully pursuing their careers as performers and teachers. As they grew, Maharajji included them in his tours in India as well as abroad. He established Jai Kishan at Kathak Kendra while Mamta and Deepak work at Kalashram as senior teachers. Theirs is a rich legacy, laced with years of pursuit and perseverance.

A scene from Kathak Yatra.

Photograph courtesy: Dinesh Poddar

KALASHRAM
HIS DREAM

When Maharajji was working at the Kathak Kendra, he spoke about how he wished to create an institute with a natural environment, where students could feel the rural flavour of India and enjoy all the goodness of nature. While living in Delhi this was near impossible, but he still wanted to create such a place that would allow students to interact and share the beauty of natural surroundings. According to his vision, the teaching curriculum of this institute would inspire the students to learn and appreciate music, dance, theatre, painting, literature and other allied arts. He strongly believes that an artist can be successful only when he or she draws inspiration from various art forms.

His dream, Kalashram, has been in operation since 1999 and will soon have its own building at Gulmohar Park, New Delhi. Plans are under way to have an amphitheatre, dance and music rooms, a studio for rehearsals, audio-videography space, a library, archive and research rooms, space for yoga and meditation and so on. There will be *baithak*s (interactive sessions), lecture-demonstrations, talks and seminars and small presentations held on a regular basis.

Lost in abhinaya. Photograph: Avinash Pasricha

A pose suggesting an offering to the gods.

Clockwise from above: Breaking into an informal dance posture; In a park in China with Saswati; With Saswati and Mahua in Dehra Dun.

Reflecting with a half-smile on his face.

The dagger pose.
Photograph: Avinash Pasricha

At the Vasantotsava programme organised by Kalashram at Kamani Auditorium, Delhi.

Photograph: Ashwani Chopra

Birju Maharaj and Saswati with Ritu Samhara *dancers.*
Photograph courtesy: Dinesh Poddar

A scintillating performance in Kolkata with Zakir Hussain.
Photograph courtesy: Dinesh Poddar

Clockwise from above: A beautiful dance posture; Dancing at the Ananya festival at Purana Qila, Delhi; L to R: Yashaswini, Tribhuvan, Shinjini and Ragini.

Dancing at the Ram Mandir, Nasik.

Above: Three striking poses.
Left: After a performance in Beijing.

Two intense dance postures.
Photograph on the left: Ashwani Chopra

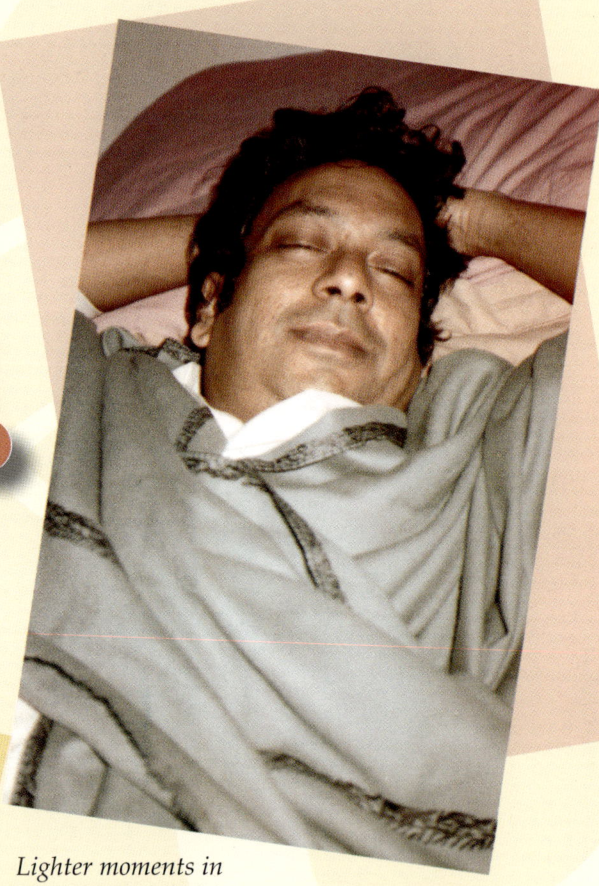

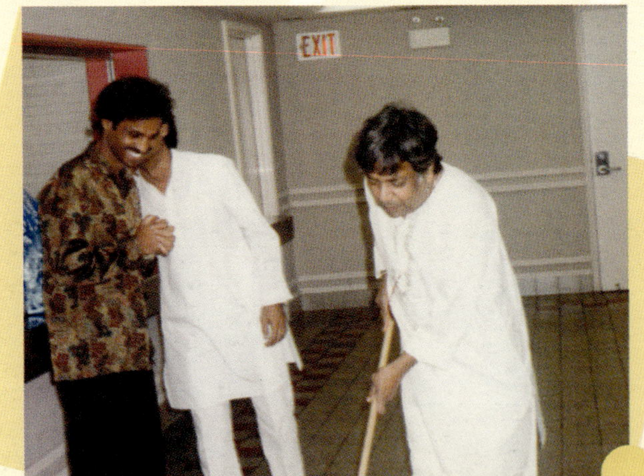

Lighter moments in Birju Maharaj's life.

Clockwise from left: Enjoying a simple meal with Renu Sharma, Uma Trigunayat, Arjun Mishra and Kiran Chauhan in Lucknow; Performing his morning prayers at home; Trying a pizza; Feeding his son, Jaikishan.

At the Konark festival organised by Gangadhar Pradhan.

Above: Having great fun on a rikshaw driven by Zakir Hussain. Right: Birju Maharaj after a dip at the Kumbh Mela.

Birju Maharaj loves being close to nature.

MANY ACHIEVEMENTS

Outreach Work

A major contribution of Maharajji's to the Kathak world has been his workshops and master classes, which he conducts across the country and abroad. These sessions provide a short span of teaching with a packaged syllabus that focusses mainly on giving the students an understanding of the subject. Initially, when Maharajji started teaching in this manner, people were apprehensive and reluctant to believe in the results, but soon this method became so successful and popular that Maharajji has been receiving requests from all over the country. The shortest duration for these workshops is two days and the longest, two weeks. However, the regular workshops that he conducts annually are for about six or seven days. These are usually held in Kolkata, Delhi, Mumbai, Lucknow, Murshidabad, Patna and Guwahati. Students from the age of six onwards, with a basic knowledge of *taal*, footwork and hand movements, are allowed to enrol. There is no upper age limit, as long as their physique and stamina allows them to learn dance. Little children, young learners, performers and teachers all learn with joy as Maharajji attends to them with individual attention.

It is hard to believe, especially for those who have never witnessed these sessions, how much the students gain from them. Learning new items, rhythmic patterns and *taal*s, experiencing the finer aspects of *abhinaya*, understanding the beauty of lines in the body, learning ways of reciting the compositions, aesthetically presenting on stage all this and much beyond, are the high points of the workshops. Maharajji does not believe in merely teaching the content; he explains the details of each piece. Working tirelessly, even at this age, he gets real joy and extreme satisfaction on seeing the results of his training. In most places the number of students coming for these sessions is huge. At the end of these sessions, the students and their guardians express deep satisfaction and gratitude. The last day of the session usually winds up in tearful farewells; the most touching moment is when the tiny tots lovingly hug him and make him promise to return soon.

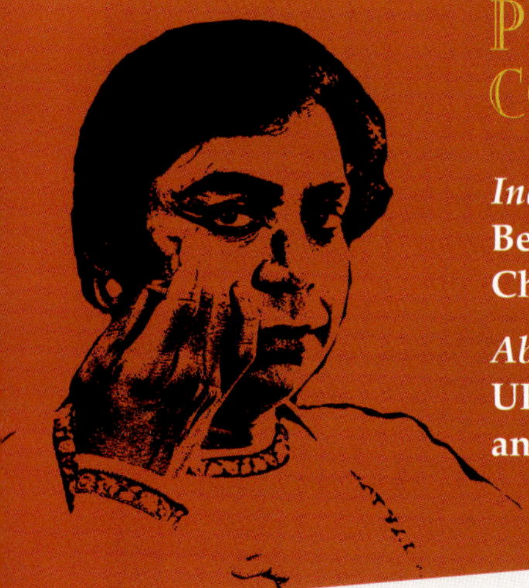

PLACES WHERE MAHARAJJI CONDUCTS WORKSHOPS

***India:* Kolkata, Mumbai, Delhi, Lucknow, Pune, Patna, Ahmedabad, Bengaluru, Guwahati, Agartala, Coochbehar, Berhampore, Asansol, Chhattisgarh, Nasik, Jammu, Jaipur and Kota.**

***Abroad:* USA—Minneapolis, Chicago, San Jose and New York; UK—London, Manchester and Chester; Paris; Japan; Malaysia; Perth and Bangladesh.**

Disciples and Associates

Pratap Pawar, Tirath Ajmani, Pradeep Shankar, Munna Shukla, Rani Karna, Prabha Marathe, Rashmi Bajpeyi, Bharti Gupta, Shovana Narayan, Hare Kishan Behra, Rekha Shankar, Krishan Mohan Misra, Ram Lakhan Yadav, Om Prakash Misra, Shivji Misra, Brojen Mukherjee, Vijay Shankar, Rekha Patki, Shraddha Dhabade, Rachna Sarang, Madhurita Sarang, Chetna Tiwari, Subhash Dixit, Vaswati Misra, Pallavi Bhagwati, Neelima Azeem, Komal Dhameja, Rupali Chakravarty, Bipul Chandra Das, Kiran Bhargava, Renuka Basu, Shobha Tripathi, Savitri, Durga Arya, Kalyani Pal, Shubha Desai, Darshini Desai, Aditi Mangaldas, Daksha Seth, Ishira Parekh, Renu Sharma, Nandkishore Kapote, Anuradha Lahiri, Sumita Dey, Ram Mohan Misra, Jai Kishan Maharaj, Ram Kishan Pande, Brij Raj, Ashok Chakravarty, Raghav Raj Bhatt, Soma Dutta, Malti Rawat, Deepak Maharaj, Mamta Maharaj, Abhay Shakar Misra, Madhukar Anand, Praveen Gangani, Pragati Sood, Kishan Kumar, Abhimanyu Lal, Kiran Chouhan, Shikha Khare, Arjun Misra, Vijayshree, Ruby, Priti Agarwal, Purnima Kharge, Sandhya Pande, Dipanwita Sinha, Sudeshna Maulick, Kakoli, Roobi, Rohini, Parna Ghosh, Mahua Shankar, Sanjeev Parihasta, Raghav Sah, Hemanta Kalita, Murari Sharan, Jayant Bhagwati, Moumala Naik, Payal Upadhyay, Parakh Madan, Utpala Kalita, Neelima Beri, Anjali Sachdeva, Sonali, Deepti Gupta, Anshu and many more.

Awards

Maharajji has received several prestigious awards and recognition, both from the Government as well as private organisations. At the age of twenty-seven he was one of the youngest to receive the Sangeet Natak Akademi award in 1964, from President Dr S Radhakrishnan. In 1984-85 he received the Padma Vibhushan from President Giani Zail Singh and became the first recipient of this prestigious award in Kathak. In the same year he was also the first recipient of the Kalidas Samman for dance from Madhya Pradesh. Sri Krishna Gana Sabha (in Chennai) honoured him with the Nritya Choodamani. He received the Andhra Ratna award from the Government of Andhra Pradesh. Benaras Hindu University, Indira Kala Vishwavidyalaya (of Khairagarh University) and Rabindra Bharati University have conferred upon him Honorary Doctorates (D. Litt). In 2007 he received the Yash Bharti award from the Government of Uttar Pradesh and, in 2008, the Vishwa Bharati University honoured him with the Desikottam award.

Maharajji has received several other prestigious awards such as the Rajiv Gandhi Peace Foundation Award, the Adharshila Shikhar Samman, the Critics' Recommendation Award, the Nritya Vilas and the Soviet Land Nehru Award. He is also Fellow of the Central Sangeet Natak Akademi and Ratna Sadasya of the Uttar Pradesh Akademi.

The French government awarded him the Officier Dans L'Ordre des Arts et des Lettres in 1995 and the Mayor of Paris honoured him on behalf of the city.

Literary and Musical Work

Blessed and inspired by his grandfather, Bindadin Maharaj, Maharajji has written over a hundred compositions. Like his grandfather he uses mostly the Avadhi dialect in the traditional compositions. Many of these are popularly used by Kathak dancers. Some have been compiled in two small books, *Brij Shyam Kahe* and *Anubhooti*. Maharajji has brought out a unique book, *Ang Kavya*—on nomenclatures of *nritta hasta*s (dance movements) of Kathak. This book not only gives names to the movements but also suggests short hand graphics for these movements. Maharajji has produced a series of seven music CDs—*Chhand Kavya,* which have musical compositions such as *vandana, shloka, thumri, dadra, tarana, ghazal, holi, bhajan, chaturang* and *kavita.* There are also rhythmic compositions in different *taal*s. In addition, there are two videos, *Kathak Parichaya,* introducing Kathak to the general masses. These have even proved to be very popular abroad.

Foreign Students

Surama Gandharias (from Uruguay), who was really my inspiration to start understanding the depth of Maharajji's training, was continuing to learn with us until her tragic death. She was found dead in her flat at Golf Links, Delhi, one morning. She had been electrocuted. Maharajji was shaken for a long time, as she was such a fine person, a great friend, a sincere and dedicated student and a lovely dancer.

Her role as Putana and Kansa, the court dancer in the dance-drama *Krishnayan*, still remains fresh in our minds. Maharajji taught her with a lot of affection and she saw in him a great mentor and a reliable friend. For some time Maharajji was so disturbed that he had illusions of her presence around him. As he is a nervous person he felt scared of certain strange sounds (rhythmic knocks and whispers) or visions such as shadows near the classroom, a bunch of hair often swirling in the corner of our class and so on. As time passed, he remembered her in his prayers and wished her soul peace. Even today we both remember her with love.

During the late seventies a young student from Guyana, Philip McClintock, came on a scholarship to learn under him. He was dark and had a strong body. Maharajji initially wondered why the boy had chosen to learn dance and how he could be moulded into the grace of the dance. The first couple of months were challenging for both the master and the student but soon Philip became the talk of the institute. Everyone saw a tremendous potential in him. His dedication was contagious and motivated his fellow students. Within a year he became Maharajji's favourite and the pride of the Kathak Kendra. He started performing in all the major presentations of the Kendra and did some powerful roles in the dance-dramas. His roles as Jatayu and Sugriva in *Katha Raghunath Ki* were remarkable. He got offers to dance in many events in Delhi and outside and Maharajji put in his total energy and creativity for his performances.

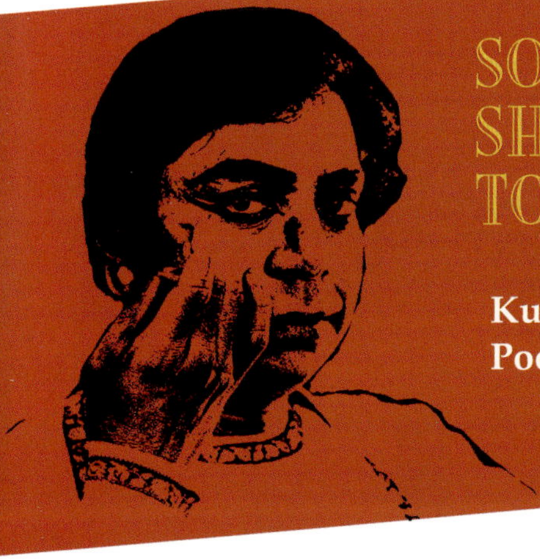

SOME CLOSE ASSOCIATES WHO SHARED IDEAS AND OCCASIONALLY TOOK SOME GUIDANCE

Kumudini Lakhia, Maya Rao, Uma Sharma, Madhavi Mudgal, Poornima Pande and Ranjana Srivastava.

When it was time for him to leave, everyone was in tears. Philip was terribly depressed and he told Maharajji that his soul would always remain at his feet. A couple of years later, Philip developed some serious kidney problems and passed away, after a long battle with the ailment. We were all shocked at the news. Looking back on those days I see a total metamorphosis of a strong and rough personality into a graceful, elegant dancer.

Around the mid-sixties, Wendy Patrik came from the USA; she was determined to learn Kathak and Hindustani music. She started taking dance classes under Maharajji and vocal music lessons from Siddheswari Deviji. She also learnt the pakhawaj from Guru Purushottam Dasji. It was a great combination of three stalwarts in their respective fields. Janaki, as she was named by Siddheswariji, was very sincere in her training and never absented herself from a single class. She was disciplined in nature, which also reflected in her learning. After her initial years of training she returned to the US for some time but came back again to pursue higher training, particularly under Maharajji. During my first visit to the US with Maharajji, in 1974, the Asia Society engaged her to be our tour manager, which was a great help for all of us.

Memories of another devoted student float in my mind—Manoranjan Joshi, a young boy from Nepal. He was of short build and had a timid nature. Maharajji loved him dearly and for the entire period of his stay Manoranjan remained totally devoted to him, spending all his time with Maharajji. He learnt under him, ran errands for him, escorted him wherever he went, almost like a Man Friday. After he left in the late sixties we did not hear from him until recently when he called from Nepal and told Maharajji that he was unwell and missed him.

Around the late seventies, a French girl, Veronique Azan, was sent by Pandit Kishan Maharaj to learn Kathak from Maharajji. Her parents regularly visited Varanasi and stayed for a few months to learn music. Her father learnt the tabla from Pandit Kishan Maharaj and her mother took sitar training from Pandit Amarnathji. Little Veronique had started learning the basics of Kathak from Alaknanda Devi and had a great passion and determination to learn properly. As she was too young to stay alone in Delhi, Maharajji's family welcomed her to live with them. Maharajji was extremely affectionate and caring towards her and tried his best to ensure that she did not miss her family. Since Maharajji's family members were vegetarian, he bought a stove, cooker and some utensils to enable her to eat non-vegetarian food, bought from outside. Maharajji would also cook eggs for her. When she grew a little older, Maharajji put her in the Kathak Kendra hostel under the care of Uma Trigunayat, the warden. However, Maharajji was always concerned about her wellbeing and instructed all of us to attend to her needs.

Veronique was a sincere and devoted student, completely immersed in her training. She had a natural talent and understanding for rhythm and a fast grasping power. Her hard work and Maharajji's training soon showed results as people started admiring her dance. She participated in most of the choreographies under Maharajji's direction and started performing solo at a young age. Veronique toured with us to various places within India as well as abroad. Though now it has been some time since she left India, Maharajji and all of us remember her fondly and hope she will come back one day.

LIST OF FOREIGN STUDENTS

Surama Gandharias (Uruguay), Numi (USA), Janaki Patrick (USA), Manoranjan Joshi (Nepal), Satnaraine Balkaran Singh (Trinidad), Nirmala and Ramesh Nandu (Mauritius), Gora Singh (USA), Martha (Argentina), Philip McClintock (Guyana), Mumtaz Ali (Guyana), Veronique Azan (France), Chandra Sukhai (Surinam), Davies (USA), Andreas (Spain), Savitta Ramjattan (Canada), Miriam Philips (USA), Kelly Lee Verma (Holland), Andreine Bell (France), Benaaz and Behbein (Iran), Ziang Zun-Shanu and Manu (China), Gion (Korea), Shibli Mohammad, Munmun Ahmad, Shajuddin Ahmad, Kochi Rehman, Tithi and Aruna Haider (Bangladesh). The more recent students from abroad are Susumu Naramura (Japan), Masako Sato (Japan), Ling Ping (China), Harri (Vietnam), Natalia Hildner (USA), Aila el adroos (Indonesia), Nikkessa Charles (USA), Lily and Annie (France), Devika Chetram (Canada) and Radha (Croatia).

Another student, Satnaraine Balkaran Singh, came from Trinidad on an ICCR scholarship to learn from Maharajji. He initially had some training from Pradeep Shankarji and was very disciplined and sincere. He had a strong physique and precision in his lines and movements. Sat, as he was popularly called, participated in many dance-dramas choreographed by Maharajji and played important roles, including Kartik in *Kumar Sambhava*.

Two Chinese students were sent by their government to learn under Maharajji for a year. One was a professional singer and the other a senior dance teacher at the National Academy, Beijing. Both were above sixty and no one could believe this as they had perfectly petite and graceful bodies. Even at that age they were so hardworking and sincere that within a short period of time they learnt a lot. They had Chinese names, which were difficult to pronounce, so Maharajji named them Shanu

SUPPORTERS FOR HIS TOURS ABROAD

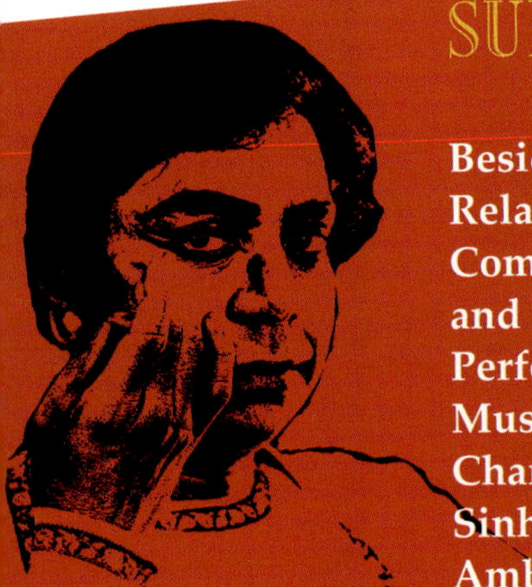

Besides government organisations such as the Indian Council for Cultural Relations, the Ministry of External Affairs and the Festival of India Committee, we have had the support of various private organisations and individuals from across the world. These include: Asia Society for Performing Arts, World Music Institute, Katha Dance Theatre (Rita Mustaphi), Trangini (Anuradha Nag), Anand Ashram (Satyanarain Charkha), Lotus Arts, Kathak Dance and Ensemble (Janaki Patrik), Anila Sinha Foundation, Chhandam (Chitresh Das), Bhairavi Kumar, Anjani Ambegaonkar and Nyssia Landsberg in the USA; Bharatiya Vidya Bhawan in the UK and the USA; Trana Dance Centre (Devika Chetram) in Canada; Sujata Banerjee Dance Company, Asian Music Circuit (Veeram Jassani), Pratap Pawar Dance Company, Sanskriti (Birendra Shankar) and Sama Arts (Jay Viswadeva) in London; Mandapa in France; Pan Asiatic Society (Allesio Alba) in Italy; Temple of Fine Arts in Australia, Malaysia and Singapore and Nrityangan (Shibli-Nipa) in Bangladesh.

and Manu. They stayed at the Kathak Kendra hostel and cooked their own food. Often they would prepare soup and vegetable momos for Maharajji to eat as an evening snack. Owing to the similarity in age they shared a very cordial relationship with Maharajji. Even beyond their class training they loved to watch Maharajji create new items and compose music. Maharajji had composed a special footwork pattern for them, which they enjoyed doing; even today this is taught as Chinese footwork (*lari*). They admired Maharajji's singing and often tried to learn Hindi songs. Their soul was really in music and when they returned to China they worked sincerely to groom young students into the art that they had learnt with such passion. Soon after they left, we had occasion to visit Beijing and were delighted to see the training they had given to the young students at the Academy.

Around the late seventies came the sincere and devoted sister-brother duo from Mauritius—Nirmala and Ramesh Nandu. Numerous other students from all over the world came to learn from Maharajji and took back lovely memories of him as a great guru.

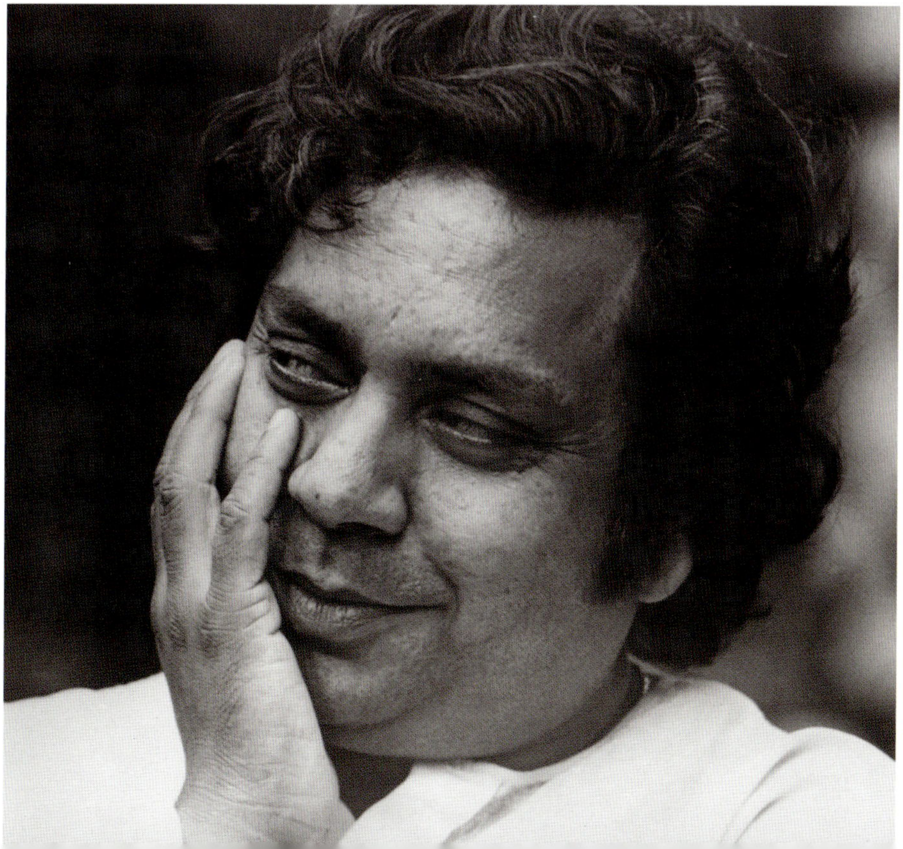

Above: After the Soviet Land award ceremony.
Right: Receiving the Padma Vibhushan from the then President of India, Giani Zail Singh.

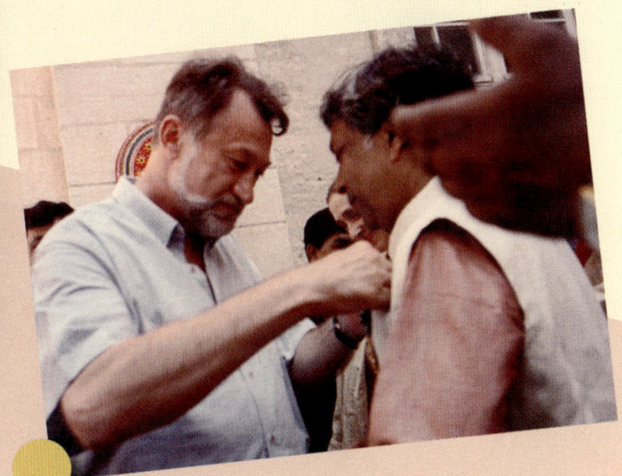

Clockwise from left: Receiving accolades from Shivraj Patil, then Home Minister of India; Being presented the Andhra Ratna award by Mother Teresa; Receiving an award in France.

Above: With disciples, Shibli Mohammad, Saswati, Malti and Kelly.
Right: With his friend, Vijay Kumar, in New York.

Clockwise from left: With Saswati and her sister Vaswati Misra; Enjoying a relaxed moment with his friend and disciple, Pradeep Shankar; His promising disciple, Philip McClintock, with Nupur Shankar.

Facing page: Kavita, his eldest daughter, in a Krishna pose.
Above: Perfection in every move.
Left: Krishan Mohan, his cousin. Photograph: Avinash Pasricha

Clockwise from left: Having fun in a park in Pune with Nand Kishore, his disciple; Vaswati Misra; With his disciple, Madhukar Anand.

Sharing a joyful moment after the performance of Shan-e-Awadh *with his disciple Surama Gandharias of Uruguay.*

Birju Maharaj's publications and releases.

संतोष
हावड़ा स्टेशन
Kathak Parichaya
An Appreciation of Kathak
Kathak Parichaya
An Appreciation of Kathak
Produced by
Pandit Birju Maharaj
Volume I

A perfect example of the guru-shishya *(teacher-student) blend.*

DIFFERENT STAGES

Productions

Pandit Birju Maharaj's numerous productions of the time since he settled in Delhi cover a wide range of themes and concepts. Some full-length dance-dramas are on traditional, mythological, historical and social themes while others are short group items, both thematic and abstract. Then there are some solo and duet choreographies which have visual beauty.

Two beautiful documentaries that capture the life and work of Pandit Birju Maharaj have been produced by the Film Division of India. The documentary made by Chidananda Dasgupta is on the highlights of the life of Maharajji, especially when he was trying to establish himself and his work. *An Illustrious Jewel* was another documentary made by VB Chandra. It brings alive the multifaceted genius of the maestro, focussing on the productions that he created during his tenure at the Kathak Kendra and Bharatiya Kala Kendra. This took almost two years to make during which time we travelled to several places that Maharajji thought would be ideal locations. The most interesting sequences were shot at Elephanta Caves, the ruins in Agra, Fatehpur Sikri, Vrindavan, Mudgaon and in the train from Pune to Mumbai.

When Maharajji joined the Bharatiya Kala Kendra he was engaged mainly in producing ballets (as these were commonly called) and teaching junior classes. His uncle Shambhu Maharajji was teaching the senior students. *Malti Madhav* was one of the first major productions that Lachhu Maharajji was invited from Mumbai to direct. By then he had successfully directed several dance sequences for films. In the lead roles were Kumudini Lakhiaji as Malti, Krishna Kumarji as Madhav and Maharajji as Makarand. The music was by the senior Dagar Brothers and the script by Bhavbhuti Sharanji.

The dance-drama, *Shan-e-Avadh,* recreated the grandeur and ambience of the era of Nawab Wajid Ali Shah and his love of music, dance and poetry as well as the lyricism of his courts. The role of the Nawab was initially played by Krishan Kumarji and later by Pradeep Shankarji. The music was composed by the senior Dagar Brothers and the script was by Shinglooji.

Kumar Sambhav, based on the famous work of poet Kalidasa, was next. This mythological dance-drama was on the life of Shiva and Parvati, the birth of their son, Kartik and the destruction of the demon, Tarakasur. Shiva was played by Krishan Kumarji for a long time but Parvati's role was played by Shaivanti Rajesh, Uma Sharma, Maya Rao, Chitra Rao and Reena Singha, respectively. A high point of the production was the famous duet of Rati-Kamdev performed by Maharajji and Kumudini Lakhiaji, which has remained almost unchallenged till today. The music was mostly by the Dagar Brothers but Maharajji also composed a few songs and music pieces. Naina Deviji designed the costumes and did the coordination for this production. Maharajji, along with the male dancers, prepared the sets, including the beautiful image of the Himalayan range, which was made with gunny bags, baskets, bamboo, cotton wool and other crude material. They worked through many nights creating the sets, painting and erecting.

The next major production was *Dalia*, an adaptation of Rabindranath Tagore's play. This was again a big challenge as the period to be recreated, the Persian-Iranian era, was important. The costumes, headgear, sets, music were all special. A portion of a boat sailing in water was also created on the stage, with the help of lights. Bharti Guptaji played the lead female role and Tirath Ajmaniji played the hero. The production was indeed very impressive.

Around the late sixties, the Bharatiya Kala Kendra decided to produce *Krishnayana*. Maharajji did both the choreography and the music for this production. He also wrote a few beautiful *pada*s (parts) and *doha*s (couplets) for it. Kavita, Maharajji's eldest daughter, played the role of the child Krishna. For the *Makhan chori* episode, they required a few children and I was selected as one of them. It was great fun watching these rehearsals. Soon I learnt almost all the dances and whenever anyone was missing I was happy to stand in for them. This was probably how Maharajji was able to assess my deep involvement with Kathak and my talent and discuss it with his friends and disciples.

After this very successful dance-drama, which was repeated at least once annually, the Bharatiya Kala Kendra took up a production based on the life and works of Mirza Ghalib, the famous Urdu poet. The title was picked up from his poetry, *Hota Hai Shab-o-Roz Tamaasha Mere Aage*. Maharajji's approach to its choreography was extremely innovative. He projected abstract feelings, moods, passion, emotions and human qualities personified through dancers. Maharajji himself played the role of *waqt* (time). Some famous ghazals and *rubai*s (Persian quatrains) include *Dil-e-Naadan* and *Nukhta Chin Hai*. The script was written by Rifat Saroshji. Though I was too young to understand the depth of the entire composition, I loved the dances and the intellectual approach. Looking back at it today, I feel the audience in those days was not prepared enough to understand its creative touch and hence it was not as popular as it should have been.

When Gopal Dasji was the Director of the Kathak Kendra (which by then had become a constituent unit of the Sangeet Natak Akademi), he inspired Maharajji to choreograph a dance-drama based on Tulsi Dasji's *Ram Charit Manas*. Induja Awasthi had written the script. This was a mega production and a masterpiece among Maharajji's works. The concept of a Sutradhar-Kathakar group was used for the first time in this dance-drama in a very aesthetic manner. Maharajji led the storyteller's team, which bound together the main story through mime, narration and dance. The characterisation was meticulously done and the production was well appreciated. Particularly impressive were Pradeep Shankarji (who played three major roles—Dashrath, Kevat and Ravana) and Philip McClintock, who marvelled in the roles of Jatayu and Sugreeva. Maharajji composed extremely melodious music. Kumudini Lakhiaji's sister-in-law, Meerabehn, designed the costumes.

The next major dance-drama choreographed by Maharajji was *Malvika Agnimitram*, a famous work of Kalidasa. I had the privilege of playing the lead role. It had a few beautiful dance sequences and a royal court dance competition. By this time Maharajji was composing all the music himself and often wrote the lyrics as well. However, the production did not make an impression.

The production that followed was another very popular dance-drama, *Hori Dhoom Macho Ri*. Celebrating the festival of colours, Holi, it was based on compositions by Bindadinji and Padmakarji. The script was written by Sarveswar Dayal Saxena. The choreography, music, lyrics and visualisation together made for a perfect annual production of the Kathak Kendra and continued this way for several years.

Almost soon after this, the Kathak Kendra took up another major production, *Roopmati Bazbahadur*, a popular love legend from the Mandu area, in Madhya Pradesh. Maharajji's choreography was beautiful; especially captivating was the music which had a blend of Rajasthani folklore and Arabic melody. Rifat Saroshji wrote the script and Kumudini Lakhiaji designed the beautiful costumes.

It was around this time that the Kathak Kendra decided to present a dance-drama on the life and works of Habba Khatun, a famous poetess from Kashmir, who wrote sensitive poetry highlighting divine love in nature. She, however, died in oblivion. During her lifetime she had to face a lot of criticism and humiliation, as those were days of strong fanaticism in religious beliefs and thus her work was considered obscene. Her poetry came to the fore and was immensely appreciated much after her death.

Maharajji then choreographed the famous work of Kavi Jaydev, *Geet Govind*. Initially the presentation had lyrics in Hindi, which were translations of the Sanskrit *ashtapadi*s (eight steps). Later Maharajji recomposed it with the original text. The music created by him for this is extremely melodious.

Simhasan, a dance-drama inspired by the *Mahabharata*, gathered mixed feelings from the viewers, while *Meera-Hari Rang Rachi*, based on the life and works of Meerabai from Rajasthan, was very well received. Nearly twelve of Meerabai's *bhajan*s were used to create the basic text, as if narrated by the poetess herself. The childhood days of Meerabai, her joy and pain, surrender and satisfaction, were all incorporated and expressed through the haunting melody of the *bhajan*s.

The short choreographies which followed thereafter in quick succession were mainly for tour programmes in India and abroad. These include *Shaahi Mehfil*, *Rajput Ramani*, *Nupur*, *Taj Mahal* and *Intezaar*, a solo composition performed mostly by Bharti Guptaji, which portrays the anguish and agony of a *nayika* (lovelorn maiden) who pines for the arrival of her beloved even after he has betrayed her. This was one of my favourite items as the choreography by Maharajji was unique; it weaved patterns of rhythmic phrases in different tempos. Along the lines of the Urdu *nazm* (a genre of poetry), it builds up the mood and excitement of the composition, ending in an emotional climax.

During the tenure of Keshav Kothariji as Director of the Kathak Kendra, several contemporary and experimental choreographies were conceived. One of these was *Laya Parikrama* (Rhythm in Universe). It was the first offbeat work created by Maharajji and its abstract approach, choreography, music and costumes were well appreciated. The success of this production set the path for several imaginative compositions, which followed in quick succession. Almost every year, during the annual Bindadin Jayanti festival, Maharajji choreographed two to three short numbers on abstract themes. These included *Ghungroo Sangeet/Tarang*, *Naad Gunjan* and *Ang Tarang/Leelangika*. *Thumri Malika* was one of the most lyrical, expressive and popular compositions based on eight *thumri*s written by Bindadinji. Through group duet and solo presentations, this item brought alive the playful interaction of the *sakhi*s (friends) and Krishna, though Krishna's presence was felt only through the imagination. *Darbar-e-Salaami* was a group dance which tries to capture the style of Kathak as performed in the royal Mughal courts.

Nritta Kelli was performed for the delegates of the Asian Games in 1982. The Kathak Kendra was asked to present a dance programme and Maharajji decided to choreograph a number based on several games that are popular in India. He represented these through rhythmic interplay and appropriate choreographic patterns; the number was highly appreciated. *Rasaranya, Yati Darshan, Kachehri Taal Vadya Ki, Antakshari, Ashta Nayika* and *Panchtatva* were some of his later compositions.

Between 1980 and the late 1990s, Maharajji choreographed a few interesting short productions with a contemporary approach. *Anamya* (pliable), the autobiography of a piece of iron ore, was one such. It was an extremely imaginative and bold attempt to reveal the helplessness of people who are compelled to conduct unlawful acts under pressure. The pain and envy of the iron piece, which cursed its life on becoming a weapon of destruction and longed to feel fulfilled and become a temple bell, a symbol of devotion and peace, was shown through the classical rhythmic strength and movements of Kathak.

Samachar Darpan (newspaper) was based on the excitement of reading a newspaper as day breaks, particularly enjoying the news of one's interest. The morning newspaper, as it arrives in a household, is in great demand—the grandfather enjoys reading about religious discourses, the son is eager to know about possible job opportunities, the father is planning his day to attend the share market with his friend, the daughter is excited to see the advertisement of her evening performance—each reviews the event of his or her interest while the newspaper is left uncared for at the end of the day.

In *File Katha* (misery of a file), which relates to a small increment for a junior staff, as it waits for years and finally tears itself apart, is interestingly portrayed. *Ritu Samhara* presents the famous work of Kalidasa; this choreography was prepared for telecast on Doordashan. In *Samanvaya* (commonness), Krishna, as described by great poets through beautiful lyrics composed in different languages, is the subject of the composition. Maharajji used the works of Rabindranath Tagore, Tyagaraja, Vidyapati, Bindadin Maharaj and many others for his compositions.

Sampadana (editing) was conceptualised by Maharajji when he was working on the documentary about his life produced by the Films

Division under VB Chandra. He had great fun on the editing table, especially when the film reels were fast forwarded, rewound, paused or matched with the music. That was when he got the idea to create this choreography and show live dancers as the editing process. It was a masterpiece and the audience went into rapturous applause at the funny moves created by the artists. Maharajji was inspired to create *Teer Tarang* (seashore) during one of his visits to Kerala. Sitting by the sea and witnessing the leaping waves running to the shore, he imagined a strange feeling between the waves, the sea and the shore. He portrayed this imaginative love triangle through dance—the possessiveness of the sea, as it feels the attraction of the waves for the shore and the sacrifice it makes for fulfilling its responsibility towards humanity.

VEER RASA COMPOSITIONS

- ***Geetopdesh*, a duet number that visualises the scene of the war between the Kauravas and the Pandavas. When Arjun loses confidence in the battlefield and surrenders his weapons, refusing to fight against his own brothers, Krishna explains to him the truth of life and the duties that one has to carry out, without bothering about the results. The lyrics are from the *Mahabharata* translated in Hindi.**
- ***Saadra*, a traditional composition written by Maharajji's grandfather, Bindadin Maharajji. The timecycle is of ten beats and the lyrics describe the scene of war between Rama and the demon king, Ravana.**
- ***Jayadrath*, an episode from the *Mahabharata*.**

Puran Katha, as the name suggests, was based on a few myths and tales from the past—the *Puranas*, the *Ramayana* and the *Mahabharata*. *Chitramala* was another interesting presentation, which was inspired by a popular television serial, *Chitrahaar*. This programme featured songs and dances from films. Maharajji decided to select some interesting sequences from his past productions and present them like a television programme. A devotional composition that Maharajji created was *Vishnu Vandana*, which he composed for Pratapji and other students. Maharajji used to watch the huge idol of Vishnu standing in all its grandeur at the Birla Mandir in New Delhi almost every day as he returned from class. He tried to capture this divine form through music and movements.

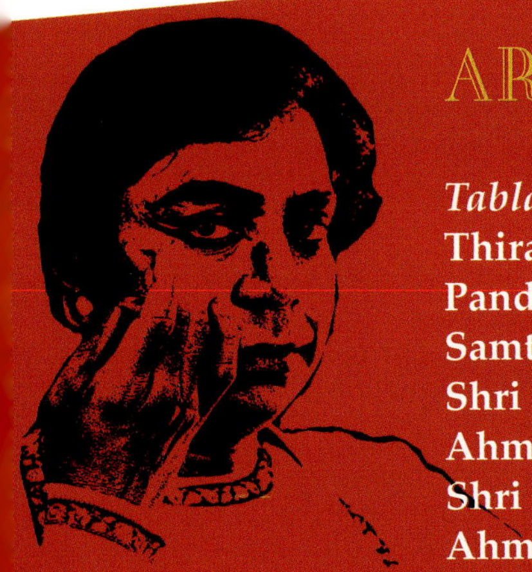

ARTISTS ACCOMPANYING MAHARAJJI

Tabla: Pandit Kanthe Maharaj, Pandit Anokhe Lal, Ustad Ahmad Jan Thirakwa, Ustad Kermatullah Khan, Ustad Munne Khan, Sheikh Daudji, Pandit Nanku Maharaj, Ustad Affaque Hussain, Pandit Kishan Maharaj, Pandit Samta Prasad, Ustad Allah Rakha, Pandit Chaturlal, Pandit Mahapurush Misra, Shri Mauji Ram, Shri Lokmanji, Shri Manika Prasad Misra, Ustad Lateef Ahmad Khan, Pandit Sharda Sahai, Shri Madan Misra, Shri Bharat Jangam, Shri Ramesh Bapodra, Shri Jagat Kumar, Ustad Zakir Hussain, Ustad Shafaat Ahmed, Pandit Kumar Bose, Shri Govind Chakraborty, Shri Ambika Prasad Misra, Ustad Sabir Khan, Shri Dilip Acharya, Pandit Swapan Chaudhury, Ustad Akram Khan, Shri Vijay Ghate, Shri Arvind Azad, Shri Mukund Deo, Shri Gopal Misra, Shri Sunil Misra, Shri Manoj Srivastava, Shri Yogesh Samsi, Shri Utpal Ghoshal, Shri Shubhankar Banerjee and Shri Debashis Mukherjee.
Vocal: Shri Harishankar Rai, Shri Jeetendra Singh, Shri Rakesh Pathak, Shri Debashis Sarkar, Shri Protip Banerjee, Shri Romen Deka, Shri Anand Gupta and Shri Anirban Bhattacharya.
Other musicians: Gopal Chakrawarty, Partho Das, Jiwan Lal, Vijay Sharma, Abdul Sami Khan, Swapnamaya Banerjee, Chandrachur Bhattacharjee, Jayanto Banerjee, Rakesh Prasanna and Jayanto Chatterjee.

His other divine compositions, both for solo and group presentations, include *Guru Vandana*, through which he pays homage to his gurus; *Krishna Vandana*, which describes and salutes the beauty of Krishna; *Saraswati Vandana*, an offering to the goddess of learning; *Aradhana*, a group choreography paying obeisance to various deities; *Aum*, bowing to the Trinity—Brahma, Vishnu and Shiva; *Shiva Stuti*, describing the beauty and grandeur of Shiva's body and adornments; *Krishna Dhyana*, the joy of a devotee as he experiences the beauty of the various incarnations of Krishna; *Kirtan*, in praise of Krishna and rejoicing the sublime union with Radha; *Ganga Stotram*, invoking the River Ganga, personified as a beautiful woman and *Dasavatar*, which portrays the ten incarnations of Vishnu and the mythical stories associated with each form. *Guru Pranam* is a composition written by Pandit Birju Maharaj and it portrays a disciple bowing at the feet of his master as he sings in his praise, describing his divine qualities.

Maharajji has also proved his mettle as a literary person, like his grandfather. Among the *pada*s he has composed, the notable ones are *Shyam Murata Man Bhaye, Sanwara Girdhar More Man Bhaye Re, Raas Rachata Brij Mein Nand Lala, Aiso Manmohan Racho Raas, Aaj Chhabi Shyam More Man Bhayee, Radherani Krishna Roop Dhari, Varanata Chhabi Shyam Sunder, Mayee Ri Manmohan* and *Man Bhaye.*

Other compositions include *Bajat Taal Dhamar (dhrupadi), Nahi Mane Ri Eri Mayee (thumri), Mora Saiyan Bhayil Beiman* and *Mein Na Manoo (dadra)* and *Bhang Peeye Khele Hori.*

Some of the songs written by Maharajji for dance-dramas are *Bin Tore Mora Lageno Jiyare (Shan-e-Avadh), Bahar Aa Gayee Lekin Na Dil Jhooma (Habba Khatun), Chalat Jaat Chitwata Brij Nari (Krishnayan)* and *Mere Chaman Mein Khile Hain (Roopmati Bazbahadur).*

Playing his grandfather, Bindadin Maharaj, in the ballet Shan-e-Awadh.

Above: Performing as the narrator in Katha Raghunath Ki.
Below: A scene from Shan-e-Awadh.

Scenes from
Holi Ayee Re.
Photographs: Ashwani Chopra

Scenes from the production, Kathak Yatra, *during a European tour.*
Photographs courtesy: Dinesh Poddar

A powerful finishing pose by Vaswati.

Scenes from
Romeo and Juliet.
Photographs: Avinash Pasricha

Performing a song on a jhula *(swing) with Pragati.*

A spectacular performance in Udaipur.

Warmly embracing sitar maestro Ravi Shankar.

TESTIMONIALS

Taal Martand—Kathak Samrat Birju Maharaj

I consider him as my younger brother, at the same time I have such regard and respect for him as one of the greatest artists in this whole world. I have always admired him since years and years, I think since he was eight years old. Today I would like to give a verbal *samman* (honour) to this great artist—I would like him to be known as 'Taal Martand—Kathak Samrat Birju Maharaj'.

Sitar Maestro Pandit Ravi Shankar, *at the Vasantotsava function at Kamani Auditorium, New Delhi, 3 February 2012*

My Mentor, My Guru

I consider Pandit Birju Maharaj as my mentor and guru...The public has great love for my art, but I am perhaps a greater admirer of his divine art.

Film actor Madhuri Dixit, *during a television show*

Golden Sunshine

Last night as I sat in the green room near Maharajji's feet, I could feel the warmth. Surrounded by people who care deeply about him, he was so much at peace—even though in physical pain he did not complain, just thanked the Lord for being there with him. The beautiful evening was one to be cherished forever. Maharajji had risen to the occasion, giving a stellar performance in spite of the pain. The three thousand-odd crowd at Shanmukhananda, Mumbai, was mesmerised. As I silently prayed for his good health, my thoughts went to 1969-70, a good forty years ago! Knowing him nearly all my life, I realised he has been an integral part of my family for three generations. As a little girl I had met Maharajji along with my parents at Ravindralaya in Lucknow. We had watched him enact *Geetopdesh* and when he depicted the Virat Roop of Vishnu, it seemed so real! During the summer holidays he would come to Lucknow to spend time with his mother; that gave me an opportunity to learn.

Even today, at the pinnacle of success, he is soft-spoken and listens patiently to all those who come to meet him. He accepts people as they are. I am privileged that his goodness has inspired me every single day. It has been a long journey from being a scared child to a keen student and finally to just being myself in the presence of my guru. Enjoying him perform, guiding him at the airport, protecting him from over-enthusiastic fans, setting the wi-fi on his iPad, changing the caller tune on his phone, requesting him to do my favourite piece on the stage, or just telling him to rest because he should—this *guru-shishya* relationship has evolved just as a beautiful sunrise—always bringing golden sunshine with it.

Renu Sharma, *disciple*

An Icon of Kathak

From the moment I became aware of Kathak, I knew the name of Padma Vibhushan Pandit Birju Maharaj—a name synonymous with the beauty and elegance of this enchanting dance form. I joined the Kathak Kendra in 1984 and soon learned that his classes were legendary and his compositions inspired every dancer, young and old. Those of us who did not have the fortune to learn directly from him would watch his disciples practise, trying hard to understand what made their dancing so rich, musical and attractive. Maharajji is a guru who transforms every student's understanding of the dance and imbues it with an aestheticism and spirituality that none of us could achieve on our own.

Maharajji's masterful use of Kathak movements and rhythm to depict images and tell endless stories is a wonder to behold. In numerous performances I have heard him say that a dancer is like a painter, painting fleeting images in time. The sixteen beats of *teentaal*, or of any other *taal*, are the shifting canvas of time on which the painter paints with his footwork and movements; each movement as passionate as the brush stroke of Van Gogh. Beyond the *guru-shishya parampara* (tradition), Pandit Birju Maharaj has redefined Kathak as a modern stage form through his timeless and breathtaking choreographies. Each of his dance creations lifts one out of this world to heights of devotion and bliss. He has composed music, written lyrics, made countless solo items and also memorable choreographic works from the contemporary to the traditional. To call him a creative genius, a veritable fount of creation, scarcely does justice to his magnificence and stature.

Deepti Gupta, *disciple*

Memorable Times

'Give me a number—any number,' Birju Maharaj said. 'Five,' I answered. 'Give me another number—any number,' Birju Maharaj retorted. 'Nine,' I said.

'OK, now you keep counting to five—again, again, again—I will count my nine with your five.' And I did, and he did.

All of us who met Maharaji after his 1963 show at Swarthmore College, a small school outside Philadelphia, Pennsylvania, were as mesmerised by his mathematical control of rhythm and endearingly jumbled English as we had been while watching his dance. Coming from a music and dance-filled childhood, I found Maharajji's art a natural extension of my dreams—his bells, gorgeous costume, expressive face, fast turns and storytelling about a flute-playing god named Krishna.

I also played the flute—I had played it since I was seven years old. And best of all, even though I was a woman, I would be allowed to wear bells, my little-girl idea of ecstatic dance finally condoned by a dance style from India named Kathak.

Naïve—perhaps. Wishful—certainly. Impractical—you bet. But that chance meeting after the performance in 1963 by the Bharatiya Kala Kendra's Kathak troupe almost fifty years ago set me on my lifelong path as Maharajji's disciple. In July 1967 I flew on Pan Am airlines to New Delhi to take an audition with Maharajji with no scholarship and only enough money for Kathak Kendra tuition and weekly room and board as a paying guest. Blind to any practical obstacles, I never considered the possibility that Maharajji might not accept me as his student. I have never asked Maharaji why he accepted me, but he did, and I embarked on my Kathak journey.

With my Kathak home in Delhi and my birth and marriage homes in the US, I have lived a divided life, spending many years of solitary practice away from my Guru's critical eyes and inspired teaching. Since retiring from the Kathak Kendra in 1998 and establishing his own Kalashram institute, Maharajji has increased his touring and teaching activities abroad. His trips to the US have given me opportunities to help arrange some of Maharajji's most memorable performances and workshops. Serving Maharajji and his art in this capacity, I have learned invaluable lessons from him and from my Guru Behen Saswatiji—Vidushi Saswati Sen—his senior-most disciple, dance partner and teaching assistant. Their increased presence in New York City has been essential in the growth of my dance company and school, The Kathak Ensemble & Friends. My students now have the benefit of Maharajji's periodic visits, seeing him and his company in performances and studying in his workshops.

Thousands of images arise in my mind's eye—of Maharajji dancing and teaching and speaking and singing and laughing—and these have kept me company and inspired my dance. I treasure these memories of his humour, of his poetic and metaphoric images, and of his eyes. Through his eyes he visualises Kathak in both the physical and imaginary realms.

Janaki Patrik, *disciple*

The Incredible Birju Maharaj

I travelled from England to India in 1958 and first met Joe from America in Mumbai, where he was on his way South to study Kathakali. But when I introduced him to Kathak and my guru, Lacchu Maharaj, he knew he must become his student too. One day, Maharajji introduced me to his twenty-one-year-old nephew, Birju Maharaj. While sharing a taxi back to the city, Birju Maharaj told me that he and his uncle, Shambhu Maharaj, taught Kathak at a college in New Delhi and that I should come and learn from them. And so, in 1960, Joe and I presented ourselves at the Bharatiya Kala Kendra. We understood that we were the first 'foreigners' to study Lucknowi Kathak so seriously and thus began two years of devoting ourselves to the Kendra's exciting world of dance, music and song. We were privileged when we witnessed solo rehearsals by the incredible Birju Maharaj as he prepared for his performances. He was always so generous in answering our questions or demonstrating a movement we were querying.

It was not all work and study, we had lots of fun too. Sometimes a group of us, including Birju Maharaj, would walk to Bengali Market for a snack and a glass of *lassi* (drink made from yogurt) and occasionally we would see a film. Somewhere along the way, Shirley and Joe became Shala and Raja, names with which we have been identified ever since. Over half-a-century ago I fell in love with India and Kathak and have shed many tears of joyful remembrance while writing these words. I am proud to say that Birju Maharaj is still a beloved friend.

Shirley, *disciple*

Gift from Nature

It is in the white light of truth and red light of emotion that I write about one of the most legendary performing artists of all time. Perhaps one of the greatest lessons I had the privilege of learning from Pandit Birju Maharaj was that 'truth remains meaningless without emotion and emotion is in vain if it is not for the sake of truth'. No one is as great a reflection of this wisdom as Saswati Sen, his greatest disciple.

If I had to explain what I see in Maharajji in one phrase it is *kudrat ki meherbani* (a gift from nature). Just as the wonder of nature lies in its secret power to infinitely create and recreate itself, so does Maharajji create landscapes of rhythm, movement, song and poetry. As nature can only be natural and complete onto itself, so does Maharajji's approach to art express an internal logic connecting tradition, history, spirituality, aesthetics and humanity.

I have often thought that even if colonialism took the Kohinoor away from India, no one would ever be able to take away India's true cultural richness, embodied by artists such as Maharajji. As his student, from the first *upaj* footwork I ever heard him dance…to the first *tihai* I ever learned at his Kalashram academy…to the first words of Hindi I ever spoke to him…to the first smiles I shared with his grandchildren…to the first *paran* he encouraged me to perform…to the first meal he had in my Peruvian-American home…to the last time I bowed my head to offer him my *pranam*—today and always, Pandit Birju Maharaj will live in his fan's, his student's and my mind and heart as a constant calling to a duty: the duty to respect his legacy by working towards perfection in what may be called 'art' by some, but what I like to call 'the way to enjoy, share and understand that which matters most in life'.

Natalia Hildner, *disciple*

My Guru, My Grandfather

It is often said to me that I am very fortunate to have Birju Maharajji as my grandfather, and I could not agree more; but as a child I was very scared of him. It was only later that I realised that I was in such awe of him that made me reluctant to even sit near him. The knowledge that my grandfather is a famous public personality, is loved and revered by many, made me fearful of committing any mistake in front of him during our routine dance classes. As my lessons progressed, I began to gain confidence and with age my fear was replaced by a carefree affection towards him. Maharajji would tell my mother to leave me at his place for a sleepover and I would be thrilled, because every extra moment that I got to spend with him had wrapped within it an unseen aspect of his brilliant persona.

As I admired the myriad colours of his genius, he gave me various lessons of dance and life in such a simplified manner that this learning process felt more like a fun-filled joy ride at the end of which I was eager for more. My cousins and I spent hours by his bedside playing games with him on those rare days when he was not touring. He narrated the witty incidents of his life, which taught us how one should approach the trials and tribulations that life puts us through by doing the *sadhana* of dance.

Even today, whenever he is free, I question him about his journey in the early days in an attempt to absorb as much as I can from his wisdom. I feel like a small vessel sitting by the shore of a vast ocean of knowledge, trying to fill in every bit of the precious lessons that he goes about distributing almost unconsciously.

His genius is not something I hope to capture in words because I am yet to understand its complete expanse; just like his dance, for which so much has been written and yet all of it falls short in describing the richness of his single move. But what I do understand in entirety is his immense love for every person around him and his giving nature. Even when he is busy in gadgets and gizmos, which he completely adores, his ears remain focussed on the footwork we are practising. Given his busy schedule, he makes it a point to take all his grandchildren out on spontaneous treats and delightful ice-cream outings.

His genius is encased in the many layers of simplicity and unconditional love that he bestows upon us. The awe, that generated fear in my young age, today produces infinite respect and affection for my grandfather who is a legend for the world but is a cherished friend and a guide to me.

Shinjini Kulkarni, *granddaughter*

INDEX

S

T

U

V

W

Y